A VIEW FROM LAND'S END

A VIEW FROM LAND'S END

Writers Against a Cornish Background

Denys Val Baker

WILLIAM KIMBER · LONDON

First published in 1982 by
WILLIAM KIMBER & CO. LIMITED
Godolphin House, 22a Queen Anne's Gate,
London, SW1H 9AE

© Denys Val Baker, 1982
ISBN 0-7183-0438-1

Photoset in North Wales by
Derek Doyle & Associates, Mold, Clwyd
and printed and bound in Great Britain by
Biddles Limited, Guildford & King's Lynn

Contents

Introduction

Land's End is probably the most famous landmark in the British Isles and every year hundreds of thousands of visitors flock down to stand awhile, no doubt suitably awed, upon this craggy finger of land pointing westwards. The end of the land is an emotive phrase: it says precisely what it means and yet – like the area to which it refers – leaves so much unsaid. Despite everything, despite all the motor cars, the tourists, the commercial trappings, the place remains mysterious, a world of its own. When we stand at Land's End, or indeed on many other hills and carns scattered about the narrow peninsula of West Cornwall, we are truly made aware of our human insignificance in the scheme of things. We are no more than the pebbles washed into eternity or ground into dusty sand.

Little wonder, then, that down the centuries this corner of England, West Cornwall, or Penwith as it is known locally, has proved fascinating to creative artists of all kinds – and writers in particular. Cornwall as a whole has drawn them, of course, but it is Land's End which seems to provide the ultimate and all-powerful magnet. Poets, novelists, critics, essayists, biographers – they have come, they have marvelled, and they have gone away elated to write about their experiences. Among them have been Alfred Lord Tennyson, Charles Dickens, Wilkie Collins, Algernon Swinburne, W.H, Hudson, D.H. Lawrence, R.M. Ballantyne, John Davidson, W.H. Davies, Crosbie Garstin, Compton Mackenzie, Katherine Mansfield, Aleister Crowley, Dorothy Richardson, Howard Spring, Daphne du Maurier, John Betjeman, C.C. Vyvyan, Hammond Innes, Winston Graham, Virginia Woolf,

Jack Clemo, Charles Causley, Dylan Thomas, W.S. Graham – the list, indeed, appears endless.

A View from Land's End is an attempt – the first so far as I know – to bring together the threads linking these and other writers with the strange area that has intrigued them all. It is in no sense meant to be an academic document studded with dates and other historical minutiae. Perhaps some day a bold historian may indeed attempt such a work – it would require at the least several volumes! When I began planning this book I envisaged dealing with perhaps a couple of dozen writers; as my research progressed that figure multiplied and quadrupled; by the time I had to finish the number of authors whom I found could legitimately be connected with Land's End had reached an astounding 200-plus. Needless to say, it has been impossible to deal with every one of them in a book of this length and even among those singled out for attention space limits have proved irksome. Nevertheless so far as has been possible this book attempts to provide a broad general survey of the literary connections of the Land's End peninsula covering from the time of a few early travellers through the increasingly active periods of the eighteenth and nineteenth centuries into the profusion in our present era.

While dealing in some detail with cases of special literary interest – such as D.H. Lawrence or Virginia Woolf – I have at the same time tried to touch on as wide a spectrum as possible of writers and writings. Unfortunately space limitations made it impossible to deal adequately with one section, the formidable range of Cornish antiquarian writers (men of the ilk of Dr Borlase, Davies Gilbert, Henry Jenner, Charles Henderson, in the past, and such as Professor Charles Thomas, head of the Institute of Cornwall, today).

That proviso made, I can only end with the hope that I may have managed to explain, at least partially, the magnetic way in which the Land's End peninsula has drawn such a vast and variegated group of writers. I hope the reader may enjoy the reading as much as I have enjoyed the writing.

Denys Val Baker

Acknowledgements

In preparing this first study of the literary associations of the Land's End area of Cornwall I am indebted to the following authors, editors and publishers for permission to quote extracts from various works: Frank Baker (*I Follow but Myself*, Peter Davies Ltd 1968, and *The Call of Cornwall*, Robert Hale Ltd 1976); Sven Berlin ('My World as a Sculptor', *Cornish Review*); Hammond Innes (*Wreckers Must Breathe* and *Killer Mine*, Wm Collins, 1940 and 1947); Charles Causley (*Collected Poems, 1951-1975*, Macmillan Ltd, 1975); W.S. Graham ('Alfred Wallis' *Cornish Review*); F.E. Halliday (*A History of Cornwall*, Duckworth & Co, 1959); M.A. Hollingham ('A Walk Round Land's End', *Cornish Review*); Bernard Walke (*Twenty Years at St Hilary*, Methuen & Co. 1935, Copyright holders: Oxfam); Noël Welch ('The Du Mauriers', *Cornish Review*); Ruth Manning Sanders ('*One and All*, Museum Press, 1951); Charles Simpson ('Cornish Landscape', *Cornish Review*); Arthur Caddick, ('Laughter at Land's End' and 'Second Launching', *Cornish Review*); Howard Spring (*My Son, My Son*, Wm Collins 1938: my thanks also to David Higham Associates); Mary Williams (*The Dark Land*, William Kimber, 1975); Kenneth Moss ('Return Visit', *Cornish Review*); Derek Tangye (*A Gull on the Roof* Michael Joseph, 1963); Bernard Leach ('My World as a Potter', *Cornish Review*: my thanks to Janet Leach); Ithell Colquhoun (*Living Stones*, Peter Owen Ltd. 1957); C.C. Vyvyan (*Cornish Silhouettes*, Bodley Head Ltd, 1924: my thanks to her literary executor); Erma Harvey James ('Rose Quartz', *Cornish Review*); R. Glynn Grylls ('Reflections on the Cornish' *Cornish Review*) Daphne du

Maurier (*Vanishing Cornwall*, Gollancz Ltd, 1967); A.L. Rowse ('Spring Afternoon at Charlestown', *Cornish Review*) Jack Clemo ('Gwindre', *Cornish Review*); Dylan Thomas (*Collected Letters*, J.M. Dent, 1966, my thanks to David Higham Associates); Frances Bellerby ('Artist in Cornwall', *Cornish Review*); D.M. Thomas ('Botallack', *The Granite Kingdom*, D.M. Bradford Barton, 1970) John Heath Stubbs ('To the Mermaid at Zennor' *Cornish Review*); Dora Russell ('Sea Magic', *Cornish Review*); John Fowles and Fay Goodwin, (*Islands*, Jonathan Cape, 1978); Nora Ratcliffe ('The Minack Theatre', *Cornish Review*); A.C. Todd and Peter Laws (*Industrial Archaeology of Cornwall*, David & Charles, 1972); Wallace Nichols ('Cornwall', *Cornish Review*); Phillip Cannon ('Cornish Opera' *Cornish Review*: Virginia Woolf (*Collected Letters* 1912-1922, Hogarth Press, 1976; my thanks to the author's literary estate); Mary Butts ('Look Homeward Angel' by permission of her executor Camilla Bagg); Laura Knight (*The Magic of a Line*, William Kimber 1965, my thanks to her literary executors); John Betjeman ('One and All', *Cornish Review*): Winston Graham ('Cotty's Cove', *The Japanese Girl*, Wm Collins 1971); A.F.C. Hillstead ('Folklore of Cornwall' *Cornish Review*), Mike Borg-Banks 'Granite', *Cornish Review*), Ida Proctor ('Turner in Cornwall' *Cornish Review*); D.H. Lawrence (*Collected Letters*, Heinemann, 1955 and 1930); (My thanks to Lawrence Pollinger Ltd, and the Estate of the late Mrs Frieda Lawrence Ravagli); Kenneth Lindley (*Coast Line*, Hutchinson 1950); I have made every effort to contact copyright holders, and offer my apologies to the one or two it has not been possible to trace and for any accidental omissions. To all my thanks.

Denys Val Baker

I

At the End of the Land

Cornwall boasts the longest coastline of any English county and within its ever-narrowing westward trend there lies an almost bewildering choice of attractions; Launceston, ancient citadel town bestriding a high hill which marks the old traditional crossing point of the River Tamar from Devon; King Arthur's Castle, that crumbling and legendary edifice which seems to grow naturally out of the jagged cliffs of Tintagel; the wild bare lands of Bodmin Moor stretching like a sea as far as the eye can see; great country houses like Lanhydrock near Bodmin and Trelowarren near Helston; haunted stretches of sand under which lie buried whole villages at Harlyn Bay near Padstow and Gwithian further west towards Hayle; the towering hermit's rock at Roche or tiny Dozmary Pool near Bolventor into which Sir Bedivere is said to have thrown the sword Excalibur; and a dozen other memorable images from the gaunt silhouette of Carn Brea above Redruth to the vast pit of Gwennap where John Wesley preached to thousands, from the ruins of a great castle like Restormel at Lostwithiel to the lonely left-over chimneys of a dozen old mine shafts around St Day, from the quiet rippling waters of the River Fowey to the wild and sea-washed point on which stands England's most famous lighthouse, the Lizard, that first welcoming light which greets sailors returning from the south.

The more one looks around the more the images accumulate so that sometimes it seems there can be no end to time. Yet an end there is, and it is that end – literally the end of Cornwall, of England itself – that is the subject of this book: the Land's End peninsula (itself the most legendary area in all Cornwall) and how in some strange hypnotic way it has captured the imagination of such a vast and varied number of writers.

Before considering the work and experiences of some of the hundreds of writers associated with the area it may be helpful to the reader to try and portray Land's End – as it was, as it is, and above all as it so often *seems*. For this in a word is the clue to Land's End: it is not just a place – it is a *mysterious* place. Strange, ghostly, haunted, solitary, menacing, brooding, awe-inspiring, weird, magical – the adjectives come tumbling out and yet somehow they are never enough. That is not in the nature of things, not on the Land's End peninsula: in a curious way although much more familiar to us it remains perversely more mysterious even than somewhere like the moon, where mankind with all its technical and scientific resources can probably find plenty of answers.

At Land's End neither the scientists nor even the archaeologists have been able to find any complete solutions – always, somehow, the ultimate truths have eluded them. Only fleetingly, as I hope to show, has the creative artist sometimes seemed if not to capture at least to hint an explanation, a *meaning* to all the mystery. This was done, for instance, by the novelist Ruth Manning Sanders (still alive at the great age of ninety and living in Penzance) when she recalled once walking out on the cliffs at Land's End in the twilight of a wintry afternoon when nothing was to be seen but the huge dim shapes of the silently withdrawing cliffs and the rhythmically winking eye of the Longships lighthouse.

It is then that the drowned sailors of the past can be heard hailing their names above the moaning of the waters. It is then that the sense of the primordial, the strange and the savage, the unknown, the very long ago, fills the dusk with something that is akin to dread. It is then that the place becomes haunted: a giant heaves grey limbs from his granite bed, a witch sits in that stone chair on the cliff ...

The whole point about Land's End is that if it was not secretive, if it was not mysterious, if it did not indeed reek of 'the very long ago', it would have little significance. It is precisely because somewhere at the back of our minds we are forever made aware that *at any moment* 'a giant may heave grey limbs from his granite bed' or even a witch appear who 'sits on that stone chair' – because of such things that Land's End has come to assume such a legendary place in our history, and hence is very significant indeed. And to prove the truth of this observation I do not think the reader needs to do anything more than travel *West of Hayle River*, to borrow the apt title of a recent book by one of our newer literary settlers, Gerald Priestland; that is, across the long flat causeway leading from Hayle to St Erth and head towards the rolling Penwith hills ahead, following the busy A 30 road which will soon breast the hill above Crowlas and reveal the majestic, glistening sweep of Mount's Bay (beneath whose waters whole forests are said still to lie buried), continuing through Penzance and out past Buryas Bridge and Drift and Cros-An-Wra towards the lonely sentinel of Sennen's Norman tower, the First and Last Church in England – on a little further until at last you reach the jagged point where the land ends and the sea begins. Or does it?

Legend has it that no fewer than 140 churches were buried in a single night by wild Atlantic waves in the thirty miles that separate Land's End from the Scilly Isles – and see, there *are* those very isles, magic and eerie lumps of more granite, more mystery, silhouetted in ghostly fashion on the horizon. Now is a time to ignore all the commercial trappings of car parks and gift shops and stand and look out instead upon one of the most breathtaking panoramic views known to man. This is it. You are at the End of the Land. And what do you feel? Almost certainly you will feel a profound and disturbing and forever inexplicable sense of mystery, aware in a way you will probably never forget of being in the heart of a very strange world indeed.

Before ever reaching the toe of Cornwall most visitors will already have been given a taste of the strangeness, the brooding atmosphere of past ages, which pervades the whole of the county. It was the famous poet Walter de la Mare who after a brief foray into Cornwall declared that he did not feel safe again until he had crossed back to Devon. This was put a little more explicitly by my old friend, the late W. Gore Allen, editor of the *Devon Journal*; 'Whenever I cross the River Tamar crossing east or west, I am surprised afresh that one of the world's least penetrable frontiers should be made evident by so small a width of water.'

It is indeed; whether via Brunel's famous old railway bridge or driving over the graceful sweep of the new Tamar road bridge the actual crossing is all over in a minute or so. And yet somehow – perhaps not as dramatically as at Launceston where that great castle looms ahead like some dire warning threat – there can still be no mistaking the way that the traveller into Cornwall is soon made aware of being *somewhere different*. You are not in some suburban Home County nor in one of the prettier West Country areas like Somerset or Wiltshire – you are in a land heavy with granite, bleak with moors, scarred by mines and claypits, above all greedily enclosed by the seas that are ever restless, sometimes tempestuously so. This is an impression that can be heightened as you cross those lonely moors where the Bodmin cattle stray freely and where it is possible to feel like being on the roof of Cornwall surrounded by silence and a sense of desolation.

It has been said of Bodmin Moor that it presents an almost brutal structure, a suggestion of petrified waves, crested at the tors, otherwise in deep wide undulations. This is the view of a local painter, Lionel Miskin, who has drawn attention to the deep recessions of ochre and golden grass to be found in wintertime and of greens in the spring that only lightly cover over a sculpture as black as iron or bronze. Everything seems darkly ominous – even the cattle on the moor tend to be black! Miskin recollects working both on the high land of the moor as well as in the valley running down to Golitha Falls and looking out on extraordinary shapes of clouds building up as if for a dark and powerful storm, seeing the shapes of rocks or hills appearing and disappearing in the clouds, the sun glinting on their surfaces like sculpture. All this makes a necessary preparation for the approach to the Land's End peninsula for, although very different in character, Bodmin Moor does share that same ultimate underlying sense of mystery.

This mystery is essential to any consideration of the Land's End peninsula in itself and here it is important first to remember that imprinted upon it must be the character of the Cornish themselves, a fiercely independent people ever aware of their great age and maturity. When the early Britons on the further side of the Tamar were still tilling soil the first settlers near Land's End were already tin mining and trading with Iberians and other Mediterranean peoples and so knew something of a more advanced civilisation (relics of which have been found in Cornish barrow graves). Some say the Cornish independence is due to the legacy of those earlier dark-haired invaders from the south, others that it was shaped by the experience of centuries of isolation set off by the Roman Conquests of the British Isles.

However this may be, one thing is certain: superstition flows in the blood of the Cornish. Rocks and stones, hills and valleys bear the imprint of men who long ago used to bury their dead beneath great chambered tombs and worshipped the earth goddess. Nowhere else in England are there such symbols of eastern rituals, but they are plentiful in Cornwall ... great slabs of granite tip tilted one upon the other, set in high places amid scrub and gorse, the treasures they once contained long rifled by barbarians and the bones scattered, they stand as memorials to a way of life whose memories still linger.

To stand beside them is to become rather like an astronaut in time, as Daphne du Maurier has commented in her perspicacious *Vanishing Cornwall*. The present vanishes, centuries dissolve, the mocking course of history with all its triumphs and feats is blotted out. Here, in the lichened stone, is the essence of memory itself. Scattered throughout the length and breadth of the Land's End peninsula these

chambers and barrows and trenches and mounds and circles
have the effect of suggesting that death, like the sea, is forever
present. There is always a reminder, on some ridge or hillside,
half concealed now perhaps by thorn or bracken, of a final
stillness waiting ...

For the Cornish, religion is bred in the bone, taking varying
forms throughout successive generations. As Daphne du
Maurier points out, the first settlers, like most Mediterranean
peoples, worshipped the Earth Mother, the fertility goddess
who brought life to the world. The granite rocks and stones
thrown up by nature in a million million years were regarded
as her handiwork, and beneath them she presided, mysterious
and dark, having power over all things inanimate and living.

The Celtic races brought a different cult, sky gods and sun
gods, spirits of trees, harbingers of the monotheistic God to
come, with Christianity making a perfect combination of
the two opposing forces, male and female. Then came the
holy men in droves from Ireland and Wales, baptising the
Cornish, who became saints in their turn, revered in their
lifetime, petitioned after death. The pagan streams and
wells were re-dedicated in their name, the hermits' cells
turned into chapels. Churches were built, the whole
ecclesiastical order came into being. The Cornish accepted
this with due reverence and obedience and yet underlying
all this conformity remained a deep sense of superstition,
half wondering, half afraid, a reliance on an old magic that
had never really died away. So spells, charms, curses,
wishes, things like that were regarded as having more
power than prayer. Certain birds were baleful, some
animals malign. The dead were not in purgatory or in their
graves but more likely to be found wandering in the hills or
calling from the sea. The elderly were witches, the young
were changelings. Knackers hammered and halloed from
the mines, piskies, the household fairies, discomfited the
home within, spoiling food, turning milk sour. No priest
had control over these beings: they came and went at will

and it was safer to placate them or cast a counter spell.

When the Reformation came and the mystique of the Mass was taken from the Cornish, images forbidden, incense and holy water banished from the churches, they sought consolation in a greater dependence upon magic than before. If the Reformed church could not satisfy their deep emotional needs and the old Catholicism with its ritual was unlawful and men could hang and burn for practising it, then unconscious longing turned to an older cult, age-long memory stirred, and the spirits that were in the sacred wells on hill tops and in groves, beneath the stone and in the hollows of the earth, gave an answer to the feeling of emptiness.

Here it is worth considering briefly the part that the Cornish language has played in the life of the Cornish people. In the Middle Ages, for instance, Cornish was widely spoken and indeed this is a period famous for the great Cornish verse drama about the spiritual history of man from Creation to the Last Judgement, the *Ordinalia*, or *Bewnans Mersysasek*. (The original manuscript of eighty-three hand-written folios of text on parchment has been preserved at the Bodleian Library, Oxford). According to the historian Scawen, the *Ordinalia* used to be performed at great conventions of people at which

they had famous interludes celebrated with great preparations, and not without shows of devotion in them, solemnized in open and spacious downs of great capacity, encompassed about with earthen banks, and in some part stone-work of largeness to contain thousands, the shapes of which remain in many places to this day, though the use of them long since gone. These were frequently used in many parts of the country, at the conveniency of the people, for their meeting together in which they represented, by grave actings, spiritual histories, personating patriarchs, princes and other persons; and with great oratory pronounced their harangue, framed by art, and composed with heroic style.

This was a great means to keep in use the tongue with delight and admiration, and it continued also friendship and good correspondency in the people.

Richard Carew has left this description:

The *guary miracle*, in English a miracle play, is a kind of interlude compiled in Cornish out of some scripture history with that grossness which accompanied the Romans' *vetus comedia*. For representing it they raise an earthen amphitheatre in some open field, having the diameter of this enclosed plain some forty or fifty feet. The country people flock from all sides, many miles off, to hear and see it; for they have therein devils and devices to delight as well the eye as the ear ...

Land's End itself was very close to one of the two most famous of these amphitheatres – the *Plain-an-Gwary*, or playing place, at St Just (the other being at Perran Round, near Perranporth). At St Just the *Ordinalia* was certainly no ordinary event: the proceedings continued for three whole days, with side shows, cock fights and other events serving as extra entertainments for the huge crowds that came to see performances in 'the Cornysh speche' of a play containing more than 10,000 lines, and necessitating a truly enormous cast of 125 characters. Considering it was written in a language without any great drama tradition the *Ordinalia* must remain something of a landmark in any literary history of Cornwall.

Sadly it must be admitted that there have been no outstanding successors, at least in the Cornish language, but it is interesting to note that in recent years there have been several Cornish operas written – even more interesting to note that all of these have been set in the melodramatic world of West Cornwall. *Iernin*, music by George Lloyd with a libretto by his father, William Lloyd, is based on the local legend of the Nine Maidens, a circle of granite boulders near Land's End – nine maidens turned into stone for dancing on a

Sunday, Inglis Gundry, a Cornish bard who has devoted most of his life to the study of Cornish music and language, is another composer who has tapped a rich vein of West Cornish lore in his works: *The Tinners of Cornwall*, as its title suggests, is about the early miners of the St Just area, and *The Logan Rock* is an attempt to recreate the world of the old Cornish 'trolls'. Then there is *Morvoren*, which was recently performed in London, whose creator, Phillip Cannon, declared:

> Opera has been in my mind ever since I was a boy in Cornwall. The Cornish part of me wanted to reveal in musical terms the fascinating hinterland where truth and legend meet, where the ancient culture and superstitions of Cornwall would appear against their true background of ruggedly beautiful coastline and wilder sea. It was this inner life, the musical inflection of Cornish speech, I felt I could set to music.

The underlying theme of *Morvoren* is the contrast in Cornish character; the home-loving chapel-going life with the wilder and more primitive which arises out of being always up against the elements, the sea and the hard life associated with it. There are many legends of mermaids to be found round the Cornish coast of which the story of the Mermaid of Zennor – associated as it is with the crying of the mermaid seen carved on the pew end in Zennor church – is the best known and one to which I shall return later in this book. Cannon used Zennor as his setting for his tale of that beautiful, unknown maiden who comes to the village but is eventually drawn back to her true home in the sea taking with her the young man who has fallen in love with her. The final scene in which the fisherman is drowned and all the warring elements combine – storm at sea, the voices of the unseen chorus of mermaids and the hymn tune by which the preacher tries to rally the frightened villagers – makes a truly dramatic climax.

As for the Cornish language itself, which so far as everyday usage is concerned died out at the end of the eighteenth century, recent times have brought signs of a significant

revival, encouraged by the county-wide Federation of Old
Cornwall Societies. Originally the revival was the dream of
one man, Henry Jenner, whose views were trenchantly set
forth in the introduction of his *Handbook of the Cornish Language*,
published in 1904.

> Why should Cornishmen learn Cornish? The question is a
> fair one, the answer is simple. Because they are
> Cornishmen. At the present day Cornwall is legally and
> practically a County of England, with a County Council, a
> County Police and a Lord Lieutenant, all complete. But
> every Cornishman knows well enough, proud as he may be
> of belonging to the British Empire, that he is no more an
> Englishman than a Caithness man is, that he has as much
> right to a separate local patriotism to his little motherland,
> which rightly understood is no bar, but rather an advantage
> to the great British patriotism, as has a Scotsman, an
> Irishman or a Welshman. The reason why a Cornishman
> should learn Cornish, the outward and audible sign of his
> separate nationality, is sentimental, and not in the least
> practical, and if everything sentimental were banished from
> it the world would not be as pleasant a place as it is.

Today the Cornish language is taught both privately and in
some schools, and there is generally a remarkable revival in
both language and culture. This has been reflected, for
instance, in the enthusiastic development of the annual *Gorseth
Kernow*, or Cornish Gorsedd. Appropriately enough, the first
of the revived Gorsedds was held in 1928 at that magnificent
memorial of past ages, the Bronze Age Circle of Boscawen-Un
near St Buryan, the very spot where it is thought likely that a
thousand years before the Bards of the whole of Britain had
gathered in a similar ceremony (in fact West Cornwall is a
favourite setting for the Gorsedds and one was held recently at
Zennor).

   The objects of the Gorsedds are to give expression to the
national spirit of Cornwall; to encourage the study of Cornish
history and the Cornish language, to foster Cornish literature,

art and music; to link Cornwall with other Celtic countries; and to promote co-operation among those who work for the honour of Cornwall. Many of the writers discussed in this book have been honoured by being crowned at these ceremonies, and it is not hard to respond to the sheer visual drama of the great gathering of bardic figures in flowing blue robes, the sound of the harp, followed by the resounding utterances of ancient rituals spoken passionately in old Cornish. This ceremonial is mainly based on the Welsh, but as has been explained by Cornwall's most famous Grand Bard, the late R. Morton Nance:

> We have added references to King Arthur as typifying the undying Celtic spirit of Cornwall, and other things of our own. Our robes are of the Welsh pattern but a headband of black and yellow distinguishes us. As Grand Bard, *Gways Myghal* originally wore his Breton robe and hood, with a leafy garland only. Since, a copper laurel wreath and a breastplate representing a Gorsedd Circle have been worn. Our banner bears the three rays symbol in yellow on blue with a bordure of the Cornish besants. Our *Corn Gwlas* is not a trumpet but an actual horn, decorated with copper fittings made by its blower, *Tan Dyvarow*. Our harpist, *Arlodhes Ywerdhon*, uses the small Irish harp instead of the large one used in Wales.

So today it is true to say that what might be called Cornwall's Cornishness is very much an upward trend, and thus an important contribution to that sense of apartness which becomes apparent the further one penetrates towards the very end of 'one of the world's least penetrable frontiers'. What, then, *is* the Land's End peninsula? It is an area of some eighty square miles, shaped a little like the toe of a boot or the claw of a hand – projecting from the rest of England rather as on a larger scale Italy does from Europe – and extending in circumference roughly from St Ives Bay and the Hayle estuary in the north-east, round through St Ives, Zennor, St Just, Cape Cornwall, Sennen Cove, Porthgwarra, Penberth,

Lamorna Cove, Mousehole, Newlyn and Penzance into
Mount's Bay and Marazion (with its causeway-joined St
Michael's Mount) on the south-east side.

Your first glimpse of the beginnings of this area will be as
you drive over the crest of the hill leading downwards from
Conner Downs towards Hayle, and if you are momentarily
inclined to imagine you are looking out upon an island such a
mistake is easily made. Cornwall is unique among English
counties in that it is built up of ancient sedimentary rocks
which were later invaded by acid igneous rocks which, after
lifting, later cooled slowly to form the granite which forms the
backbone of Land's End. As a result of this process, at one
time a considerable part of Cornwall was actually submerged
beneath the sea, including about half of the Land's End area
(the main north coast road from St Ives to St Just ap-
proximates to the old shoreline which gives some idea of the
rise and fall). So in reality the Land's End peninsula *was* an
island, and though since then the land masses have risen and
joined up, there is still at Hayle a river mouth and a narrowing
river running perhaps halfway across to Relubbus, so that it is
still not altogether fanciful to think of what lies west was an
island. Certainly it is fair to say that to a great many people
Penwith bears all the attributes of an island of infinite variety
indeed, for just as the coastal circumference I described earlier
is a breathtaking conglomeration of rearing cliffs and jagged
rocks, of huge granite protuberances broken suddenly by
exquisite, almost tropical, white sandy beaches – so, too, the
inland areas are a mass of fascinating contradictions ranging
from 2,000-year-old prehistoric villages to legendary standing
stones or Celtic crosses or ancient quoits.

Today, thanks to the National Trust, you can actually walk
the whole way round the coast from St Ives to Penzance; but
before we glance at some of the more vivid aspects of such a
journey it is well worth first looking at some of these inland
places I have mentioned, for quite often, in literary terms,
these have made their influences felt just as strongly as any
wild coastal scene. Here, for instance, is the naturalist W.H.
Hudson, writing in one of his most famous books, *The Land's*

End, of a day when he climbed high up on the brown moors above Zennor. As he tried to shelter himself from the fury of the wind among the large black masses of granite, the scene he looked out upon was 'exceedingly desolate', and he was glad to return to the shelter of his snug cottage. However as he lay in bed that night:

> The wind increased in violence making its doleful wailing and shrieking noises all round the house and causing the doors and windows to rattle in their frames. In spirit I was in it, out on the hillside where the birds were in their secret hiding places, in the black furze and heath, in holes and crevices in the hedges, their little hearts beating more languidly each hour, their eyes glazing until stiff and dead they dropped from their perches. And I was on the summit of the hill among the rude granite castles and sacred places of men who had their day on this Earth thousands and thousands of years ago.
>
> Here there are great blocks and slabs of granite which have been artificially hollowed into basins – for what purpose, who shall say? The rain falls and fills them to the brim with crystal clear water, and in summer birds drink and bathe in these basins. But they were doubtless made for another, possibly some dreadful, purpose. Perhaps they were filled from time to time with the blood of captive men sacrificed on the hilltop to some awful god of the ancient days. Now it seemed to me, out there in spirit on the hill, that the darkest imaginings of men – the blackest phantom or image of himself which he has sacrificed to – was not so dark as this dreadful unintelligible and unintelligent power that made us, in which we live and move and have our being.

Hudson may well have been thinking of one of the many hill forts of the early Iron Age which are a familiar feature of the Penwith landscape, places like Chun Castle near Madron or Castle-an-Dinas at Nancledra. The most famous of these sites, now a National Trust property, is Trencrom Hill which offers one of the most magnificent viewpoints in the whole of the Land's End peninsula: glimpses of St Michael's Mount and Mount's Bay to the south and the wide sweep of St Ives Bay and Godrevy Lighthouse to the north, the flatness of Hayle estuary to the east and the rolling hills of Penwith to the west. If there is one spot in the whole of Penwith where an individual might most immediately get the *feel* of the place, then perhaps it is Trencrom.

In technical terms, according to a Cornwall Archaeological Society booklet, the hilltop consists of a single massive wall utilising natural rock outcrops for much of its oval outline and enclosing an area 450 feet north-south by 300 feet east-west. There are more than a dozen hut circles within the fort, a well (probably ancient) in the site of a rocky outcrop just outside the defences to the northwest, a narrow cleft in the rocks giving concealed access into the fort, and surface finds of stray pottery suggest that it goes back to 200 BC.

However when you are standing on top of Trencrom with the wind whistling around you and great clouds ballooning across the vast sky, it is unlikely that such mundane facts will strike you as forcefully as the volume of popular legends that have grown up around Trencrom. How it was here that the giants of old used to gather – how when in playful mood they would hurl 'stones' across at their fellow-giants living over at St Michael's Mount in Mount's Bay, a distance of about five miles – yes, these are the sort of images that fit more readily into one's mood when standing on top of Trencrom, or for that matter any of the other great hills of Penwith. For, of course, we are now touching once again on the *secret* side of the Land's End peninsula: the sort of thing that persistently defies explanation, whether in detailed scientific or more sympathetic archaeological terms. Alone on top of Trencrom you will be in a mood to believe in 'giants and ghosts and ghoulies and things that go bump in the night'.

Hill forts and castles on lonely hilltops are not the only aspect of inland Penwith which have struck literary visitors. There are many other remnants of monuments which add to the district's vivid sense of past age. For instance, there are the quoits, those strange, often colossal stones which usually mark the site of a tomb: Zennor Quoit is 18 feet long and 9½ feet wide and covers a chamber formed by five large upright stones; Lanyon Quoit, near Madron, has its 17 feet capstone resting on three 5½ feet uprights. Stone circles are another striking feature, perhaps the best known being Boscawen-Un, near St Buryan, where there is a geometrically constructed ellipse with all nineteen stones standing and a leaning-off central pillar, the greatest diameter being 80 feet (it was here that the first Gorsedd of the Bards of Cornwall was held in 1928).

Then there are holed stones, such as Men-an-Tol above Morvah which consists of a large wheel-shaped stone pierced by a round hole 20 inches across and set on edge in line between two short pillars – a grown human being can actually crawl through the hole! There are, too, the *fougous* (the Cornish word for cave), low passages walled with dry masonry and reefed with large stone slabs, relics of the Iron Age: the Ministry of Works cares for one of the best preserved sites at Carn Euny, near Sancreed.

Finally, of course, there are the ancient villages which have been excavated, the most famous of these being Chysauster at New Mill, beautifully maintained by the Department of the Environment and comprising eight houses ranged in pairs along a village street. Most of the houses have been excavated to show hearths, drains, etc., and to visit Chysauster or one of the other ancient settlements such as Porthmeor, near Gurnard's Head, is to be made powerfully aware that you are now in a place where other worlds and other lives are still very much a presence.

Another aspect of the inland areas of West Cornwall which have often profoundly influenced writers is provided by the still physically visible remains of old mines, a notable example being Ding-Dong, high up on the hills of Penwith midway between Penzance and Gurnard's Head, its tall, crumbling chimney rearing up in lonely splendour as a memorial to the once active life that throbbed away in the earth below. In the nineteenth century there were literally dozens and dozens of tin and copper mines operating in West Cornwall alone – several hundreds in Cornwall as a whole – and there are many examples of writers venturing down them, and then vividly recording their experiences.

One of the great popular storytellers of his day, R.M. Ballantyne, author of *Coral Island*, was among these writers; his record can be found in *Deep Down, A Tale of the Cornish Mines*, written around 1868 when he had settled with his wife in Penzance. Ballantyne was originally drawn to the idea of writing an adventure story about Cornish smugglers (another feature of West Cornwall history) but after being invited by the manager of Botallack Mine to pay a visit he became fascinated by his experience of clattering in a little truck through tunnels carved from hard rock.

It was an eerie experience, Ballantyne recalled. Each time the vehicle stopped he could hear the dull thuds of miners striking far along the echoing galleries, and he could hear too the constant sound of trickling water for part of the Botallack Mine consisted of galleries which actually ran out beneath the Atlantic Ocean. For a writer such as Ballantyne, there was immediate appeal in the idea of a mine as the setting for a rattling good adventure yarn. Day after day he went below the ground chatting to the miners and learning the geography of all the tunnels and galleries and then he invented a lively tale of battles fought in subterranean darkness between smugglers and revenue men – with virtue triumphant in the end, of course.

In more recent times one of our great contemporary adventure novelists, Hammond Innes, used a similar setting from the St Just mining area for his novel *Wreckers Must Breathe*, capturing for us the strange desolation of a mine even *above* ground.

This is the most God-awful place. These Cornish mining villages are so drab and the coastal scenery so colourful. Today for instance as I pottered around the cliffs looking at the mines the sea was a brilliant turquoise blue with a white edge where it creamed against the cliffs. It reminded me of the Mediterranean except that the coast here is much more ragged and deadly looking. There is no opportunity to forget I am in the mining district of Cornwall. There is open ground on the other side of the road and it is dotted with grass-grown slag heaps, piles of stones which were once miners' houses and ruined chimneys that acted as flues for ventilation shafts to the mines. This is what I look out on from my bedroom window. And, believe me, when it rained this evening it looked a scene of utter desolation. It is getting dark now and I'm writing this by the light of an oil lamp. A sea mist has come up and the lighthouse at Pendeen Watch is moaning dismally. However, when it's fine it is possible to see right across the cliffs and I can just see the top of Cape Cornwall ... and from the window you look up to the slope of the moors to the huge pyramid heaps of the china clay pits.

It is perhaps worth adding here, briefly, a reminder that Jack Clemo, one of Cornwall's native-born modern poets – some would say of genius – has also captured most vividly this weird feeling occasioned in the observer by the combination of nature and man's intrusion, recalling how he was well into his teens before he realized there was something indeed symbolic about the scarred and eerie landscapes that result. All the strong and lonely idiom seemed somehow in keeping with his spiritual needs. Year after year he found himself watching, fascinated, the clayland dawns and sunsets, the first golden rays of the sun striking the white peaks, setting the metal prongs and top wires glowing and shimmering while the gravel bulk remained in shadow, and then at evening the daylight faded mysteriously from the blurred, grey masses and the weird, spiked clusters of stacks. So many different features were revealed, some magical, some terrifying, somehow free from the over simplification and sentimentality of the conventional poet's world ...

If the interior of the Land's End peninsula can possess such dramatic qualities, then what of the exterior? Here perhaps we come to the centre of our theme for though indeed there are inland marvels and mysteries – cromlechs, carns, quoits, castles, forts, monuments, mines – these are all essentially inanimate objects (even though indeed they often may seem to exude subterranean moods and sensations of the past ages). But along the wandering wind-swept, sea-washed coastline there is present another element altogether – the land yes, but the land *and* the sea: a sea that is a living, moving thing, capable of erupting as violently as any volcano, of changing from a placid blue calm of a millpond to a raging wild grey-green maelstrom of malevolence. No wonder that John Ruskin was moved to eloquence on looking at Turner's epic painting 'Longships Lighthouse, Land's End':

It is full of the energy of storm, fiery in haste and yet flinging back out of its motion the fitful swirls of bounding drift, of tortured vapour tossed up like man's hands, as in defiance of the tempest, the waves like a great army defeated by the walls of rock and beaten back until the whole surface of the sea becomes one dizzy whirl of rushing, writhing, tortured undirected rage, bounding and crashing and coiling in an anarchy of enormous power ... At the Land's End there is to be seen the entire disorder of the surges, when every one of them, divided and entangled among promontories as it rolls, and beaten back post by post from walls of rock on this side, and that side, recoils like the defeated division of a great army, throwing all behind it into disorder, breaking up the succeeding waves into vertical ridges, which in their turn, yet more totally shattered upon the shore, retire in more hopeless confusion, subdivided into myriads of waves, of which every one is not, be it remembered, a separate surge, but part and portion of a vast one, actuated by eternal power, and giving in every direction the mighty undulations of impetuous life, which glides over the rocks and writhes in the wind, overwhelming the one and piercing the other with the form, fury and swiftness of a sheet of lambent fire.

Or as another eminent critic, John Forster, expressed himself after seeing the real thing:

> Land and sea yielded each its marvels to us; but of all the impressions brought away, of which some afterwards took form as lasting as they could receive from the most delightful art, I doubt if any were a source of such deep emotion to us all as a sunset we saw at Land's End. There was something in the sinking of the sun behind the Atlantic in the autumn afternoon, as we viewed it together from the top of the rock projecting furthest into the sea, which each in his turn declared to have no parallel in memory.

This is what happens when mere mortals, even great literary figures, wander off along that ever-changing, ever-restless, ever-mysterious line between sea and land which marks the boundaries of this strange tip of England. Little wonder that West Cornwall is full of ghostly legends about the sea! At Porthcurno, for instance, when evening mists are rising it is said a black, ghostly square rigger comes sailing in from the sea and glides up over the sands to pursue its course across dry land ... many people claim to have seen the phantom ship and avow it always foretold misfortune.

Then again, around the district of St Levan storm winds have been said to embody the spirits of drowned sailors 'hailing their own names' while Newlyn fishermen were reputed to be the last in Cornwall to give up the practice of throwing fish into the sea as offerings to the sea spirits. These spirits were known by the Cornish as *bucca-dhu* (the black spirit) and *bucca-gwidden* (the white spirit) words probably akin to the Irish *puca* and the Welsh *pwca*, both deriving from the English *puck*; *bucca* is today applied jokingly to a scarecrow, but the farmers who use it are likely preserving a much older terror. The sea, with its strange lighting effects in certain

weather conditions, has encouraged many ghost stories. As
A.F.C. Hillstead recounted in 'The Folklore of Cornwall':

> A man from St Ives met a seaman and being sociable he
> tried to start a conversation but could get no response. At
> last the silent mariner disappeared and his inquisitor
> realised that he had been speaking to a ghost. He fell ill for
> six months and during that time all his hair fell out; when
> he began to recover, though, his hair grew again, thick and
> brown, as the drowned sailor's. Another story tells how
> above the grave of a drowned seaman, near Land's End, a
> ghostly bell rings from the tombstone at certain hours. A
> sceptical sailor who visited the grave and, to his horror,
> heard the bell, put to sea that same night and was never
> heard of again.

Granite is one of the keys to any understanding of the Land's
End peninsula. It is granite that forms the craggy, often awe-
inspiring vistas of the coastline, granite which heaves up
garishly to create those almost human shapes of carns and
cromlechs on the hilltops, granite indeed upon which many an
inquisitive intruder has laid hands and received strange
intimations of the past, of other ages – as it were, pulsating
through the stone.

Many writers in the past have written vividly about this
aspect of Cornwall, this stone-world – poets like Swinburne
and Tennyson, novelists like Ballantyne and Wilkie Collins,
travellers like Kilvert or Daniel Defoe, and more recently John
Michel, famous for his book *Atlantis*, but also author of a
fascinating study of *The Old Stones of Land's End*. An unusual
literary cameo of this subject was once provided by Mike
Borg-Banks, one of Britain's leading mountaineers, writing in
the *Cornish Review* about a typical cliff climb out near the
Logan Rock:

> Because the tide was low we were able to get right down to
> the very bottom of the climb at the base of the cliffs.
> Although the surface of the sea was smooth on this sunny

windless day, great long oily rollers were sweeping in. They pounded themselves into surf on the sands and thundered against the outcrop of rocks on which we were standing. The granite we were to climb rose sheer above for some 250 feet before its tooth-like summit made a cruel silhouette against a metallic sky. As I approached the first pitch of the climb, I felt again that cold pang I have come to know so well, almost to expect, at this stage. In the presence of such an ageless and immutable massif, I experienced a deep feeling of inferiority and impotence, as if it were an impertinence to sully these dignified granite walls with climbing boots and festoon them with ropes. But the feeling is transient in the face of the reality of the rock. The eyes and spirit were torn from the soaring heights to the very material problem of negotiating the first pitch. This was in the form of a crack in the cliff wall sufficiently wide to admit a man's body. I squeezed into this tomblike cavity made chilly by the morning tide. The granite here was washed hard and smooth by the ceaseless action of the sea and consequently presented an utter lack of help. It was a worthy start to a worthy climb.

Borg-Banks goes on to describe how as he climbs higher so all apathy and apprehension vanish, while the granite, now being above high water mark, changes from its cold slippery texture to that of rough fawn rock, mottled with lichen.

I was now striking form and the rough granite cliff unrolled in front of me like a dappled carpet. It was the mood that makes one relish difficulties so that the granite that looked so forbidding from below now appeared to be smiling and encouraging me. I suddenly became conscious that the noise of the surf had mellowed and a gentle breeze was fanning my cheek. Only then was I aware that I had ascended about 150 feet, the rollers creaming far below me. It is not uncommon for the climber, to become so engrossed in the technical problem of grip and balance as to be oblivious of height ...

Concluding his account with finally reaching the summit – 'I felt that tremendous wave of exhilaration and triumph that follows moments of great mental strain and physical effort, a rare and indescribable experience that justifies the risk of the climb, the reward of the ascetic' – Borg-Banks uncovers for us yet another corner on the endless mosaic of the mysteries making up the mystical world of Penwith. No wonder one of our contemporary poets, John Heath Stubbs, who lived for some years in a cottage on the cliffs out at Gurnard's Head, was prompted to write:

> This is a hideous and a wicked country,
> Sloping to hateful sunsets and the end of time,
> Hollow with mine shafts, naked with granite, fantastic
> with sorrow ...

Not everyone, of course, has the time or strength to walk the entire way round the Land's End peninsula. But certainly some parts can be explored fairly easily and are well worth the trouble. Like the walk from St Ives out past Clodgy Point towards the wild moors and sea cliffs of Zennor where alone in desolation the wanderer can feel almost like an intruder in another world. Set in the bleak and harsh though extremely beautiful moorland setting of the north-west coast of Penwith, Zennor is not the sort of place easily forgotten. Somehow it stamps its elemental image upon the mind rather like a painting or a photograph might do – perhaps more accurately one might suggest it penetrates into the consciousness.

There are many reasons for this: the more immediate and obvious ones like the physical structure of the setting, great craggy carns rearing up in several directions pointing implicitly skywards to that further mystery; and then the contrast, the neat, small fields with their Cornish stone hedges sloping ever downwards to the purple, heathered cliffs and the raging seas that have only too often spewed pathetic shipwrecks on to the sharp-fanged rocks that lie in waiting far below. And then, perhaps arising directly out of this sense of the elemental, there are more strange reasons – a sense of something weird and ghostly, of other-worldliness, in fact.

Small wonder that Zennor figures prominently in Cornish folklore. It is at Zennor that you will find a strange formation called the Witch's Rock, which once marked the Midsummer Eve meeting place of Cornish covens. Touching the stone nine times at midnight was regarded as an insurance against misfortune. Aleister Crowley, 'the Great Beast' as he himself liked to be called, was the author of several books about witchcraft and became notorious for performing Black Masses, some undoubtedly inside the beautiful old Norman Church which is a centrepiece of Zennor village itself, a cluster of houses nestling down in a sheltered valley. Like many Cornish villages, Zennor has its church set right beside the local pub, in this case the Tinner's Arms.

At Zennor Church is immortalised another famous legend which adds to the strangeness of the whole area. Apparently for many years a beautiful woman used to attend the church services, never ageing and captivating men with her beauty and exquisite voice. People who watched her leave the church said they had never seen her pass beyond Tregartha Hill and no one knew where she lived. One day this mysterious figure met Matthew Trewhella, the churchwarden's son, and the finest singer in Zennor – they fell in love, left the village and were never seen again. Some years later a mermaid hailed a ship off Pendower Cove – when the Zennor folk heard of this they assumed the mermaid to have been that strange lady in her true form, having enticed Matthew Trewhella beneath the waves.

To commemorate her they carved her image in holy oak on part of the chancel seat in the transept, depicting her with waist-length hair and a scaly tail, holding in her hand a mirror and comb (her shape is also carved on the dial of the clock). Since then the idea of the Mermaid of Zennor has been featured in many stories and poems and songs, and, of course, in Cannon's opera – all of which has helped to make Zennor rather more well known than most Cornish villages. Perhaps, too, its strong connections with the literary world have helped; in another chapter I describe in some detail the visitations of

D.H. Lawrence, Katherine Mansfield, Middleton Murry, Virginia Woolf and others.

Altogether Zennor is a most remarkable corner of Penwith ... but in the long run all its charm and impact come back dramatically to that basic sense of the powers of the elements. This feeling has been expressed vividly by a Cornish painter, Margo Maeckleberghe, who keeps a studio high up on the Carn at Zennor, and has noticed how the peculiar clarity of light throws this landscape into sharp perspective. She sees it as a land of great antiquity, primeval and sometimes savage, and believes that though her drawings *seem* to lay bare the bones of the landscape like a map of some strange country in fact they only partially build an image – it can never be the complete image.

Some further idea of the atmosphere of that remote stretch of the North Cornish coastline has been given by M.A. Hollingham in 'A Walk Round Land's End', an article I published some years ago in the *Cornish Review*.

This loneliness gave us a sense of isolation that was to last throughout our walk and open our eyes to an altered perception. We began to feel that we could walk like this forever, never having to turn back but always going on to see what was round the next headland, and the next and the next. But at the same time as scene after unsurpassable scene piled one on top of another we wanted to cry out 'Stop! It's all too much, we can't take any more.' We could have spent days, weeks, exploring any one of a thousand places, letting every facet of its magnificence seep slowly into us ... If you walk through the mining country south of Pendeen Watch, past the old and crumbling engine houses at Geevor, you can feel the earth's sadness where it has been so pierced and wounded that its seeping blood stains red the sea around the rocks of the Averack ... And then when you reach Land's End the paths are easy to follow and if you walk up from Sennen Cove the commercialisation sinks into the insignificance it deserves. You can ignore it, and once it is passed you find yourself in a fantastic land where massive, squared, granite boulders rise from the sea piled crazily against the cliffs like a set of giant child's bricks, half-collapsed and forgotten in a corner. Some of these boulders balance improbably on high ledges; others have been weathered into weird stacked formations, morticed so perfectly by the eroding wind and rain that it's hard to believe it wasn't some long forgotten and prehistoric hand that deliberately placed them there. Such an ample repayment for the effort of walking a few easy miles ...

From St Ives to Land's End, of course, is only half the story. Beyond Land's End with all its marvellous array of famous rocks named romantically the Armed Knight, Dr Syntax, Enys Dodman, there are miles of some of the most beautiful cliff scenery surely anywhere in Europe. Fortunately for the sightseer, the National Trust footpath follows this faithfully so that you can drop down into the marvellous cove of Nanjizel with its wild rocks and then climb round to Porthgwarra where the way to the sea leads through a hole in the cliff –this by the way, marks the turning point from west to south on the English coastline): on and on past St Levan Church and suddenly you are upon the startling sight of the open air Minack Theatre incredibly hewn out of the sheer granite sides of the cliff – across the bay the white sands of Porthcurno and the famous Logan Rock: after that headland leading past tiny Penberth Cove and its doll-like fishing boats pulled up on the slip and along mossy cliff tracks past the newly erected Tater-Dhu lighthouse (and incidentally on the way going close to the homes of the two best-seller authors, John le Carré and Derek Tangye) and then down into one of Cornwall's most renowned beauty spots, Lamorna Cove, home of many artists and writers.

When we reach Mousehole and Newlyn we emerge from more rural parts and enter a cluster of large villages and a major town – and these, too, of course, play an important part in colouring the character of the area. The Land's End peninsula has three main towns, each with surrounding environs of two or three large villages. These towns are St Just in the north-west corner, St Ives in the north-east corner, and Penzance in the south-west corner. Of these towns, Penzance – *Pen-sans*, the holy head – is far and away the largest and indeed today has the highest population of any single town in Cornwall, excluding the urban complex of Camborne-Redruth, which is really two towns run into one.

As might be expected, the history of Penzance is intricately woven into the whole pattern of the history of Land's End itself. Marazion, a few miles away, can actually boast of becoming the first local borough (in 1595) but Penzance only had to wait a further nineteen years for King James I to grant its charter of incorporation and from then on the town quickly out-prospered all potential rivals to become the undisputed metropolis of West Cornwall. Today Penzance, built on the side of a hill on the north-east shores of Mount's Bay so that it offers splendid panoramic views across the sea as far as Lizard Point, remains the pleasant and attractive market town it always has been. Apart from Market Jew Street, the steep backbone of the main town (with the statue of the town's most famous son, Humphry Davy, looking down upon the busy shoppers) there are many fascinating old side streets like Chapel Street and Causewayhead, full of atmosphere, while the semi-tropical Morrab Gardens are enhanced by delightful surrounding rows of Georgian houses.

The real colour and romance of the town's life story belongs to the past: as, for instance, 1595 when a squadron of Spanish galleys appeared off the coast and 200 soldiers landed at Mousehole and stormed up the hill to Paul, burning the church there and proceeding to pillage Newlyn before moving on towards Penzance. Fortunately the doughty Sir Francis Godolphin was in charge of things at Penzance and with the aid of a motley band of militia and fishermen he managed to save the day and rout the Spaniards.

Unfortunately, being so exposed on the very toe of the land, the Penzance area was forever liable to attract potential invaders and there are records of pirate raids not only by Spaniards, but also by Algerians, French and even Turkish

forces. It is to these events, and of course various more lawful
visits by many foreign boats, that historians have attributed
the scattered but persistent presence of unusually dark, gypsy-
looking local inhabitants, particularly at Newlyn, the main
port. After Penzance, the nearby villages of Newlyn and
Mousehole strike the visitor as altogether more picturesque
and ancient, both being built up the steep sides of hills with
winding, cobbled lanes lined by heaped-up rows of
fishermen's cottages.

Newlyn is now the second largest fishing port in the whole
of the West Country (after Brixham) and it is a beautiful sight
on a sunny day to look down upon the harbour crowded with
row after row of 60- and 90-feet fishing boats painted in bright
blues and whites or greens and yellows and greys and reds,
their masts swaying and rattling in the breeze. Mousehole is
much smaller, a port so minute that each winter the
authorities are able to close the harbour entrance against the
rough seas with slotted wooden timbers, but like Newlyn it is
rich with history. Both Mousehole and Newlyn – especially
the latter which is the home of the famous Passmore Edwards
Art Gallery – have strong local groups of painters and
craftsmen.

If we move from south to north and St Ives, then we move
from the purely picturesque and quaint to something rather
more special for here is a town which has often been described
as the jewel of the Cornish Riviera – a remark which in all
honesty I should qualify as applying rather to the general
setting of the town rather than to its central quarters which
alas have by now been somewhat ruined by gift shops, 'caffs'
and other slightly tawdry-looking establishments catering
frenziedly for the tourists. No matter, nothing can ever take
away from St Ives its breathtaking and beautiful scenery – no
one is likely to forget either driving down Tregenna Hill or
leaning out of the little shuttle train from St Erth and having a
first view of the huge white sands of Porthminster Beach
leading on to the high-walled harbour and the old
'Downalong' fishermen's part of St Ives – and then above the
harbour that strange hump of land known to all and sundry as

'the Island', on top of it perched the tiny chapel of St Nicholas – finally, beyond the Island, the most magnificent beach of all, Porthmeor, famous for its surfing on the great Atlantic rollers endlessly pounding their way over the sands (until at certain tides they wash right up against the houses and artists' studios lining the beach – hence the title of one of my own earliest autobiographies, *The Sea's in the Kitchen*; it literally was, frequently!).

St Ives is a place of whiteness and lightness and wonder, so it is hardly surprising that over the years it has become perhaps our most famous art colony outside of London. This has been the world of Alfred Wallis, of Ben Nicholson, of Peter Lanyon, of Barbara Hepworth, of Bernard Leach, of Robin Nance – artists and craftsmen whose work is to be found in galleries and museums all over the world. It has many literary associations, too: Virginia Woolf spent her childhood at Talland House which looks out over St Ives Bay to distant Godrevy; she used Godrevy as the model in her famous novel *To the Lighthouse*; and, as I have mentioned, D.H. Lawrence and many other well-known writers lived just a few miles away. So in its own way St Ives may be said to have made a unique contribution to the character of our Land's End peninsula, flavouring its mystery and sense of past with the colour and gaiety of modern artists at work – yet of course they, too, inevitably have been profoundly affected by their elemental surroundings.

Finally, we have St Just and adjoining Cape Cornwall, England's *only* cape. This is certainly the town most totally buried deep in the world of Land's End, which lies only five miles away. St Just seems to have by-passed all change; one has the feeling it has existed forever, standing in the strangely shaped main square an ugly yet somehow haunting juxtaposition of huddled grey granite miners' cottages and pubs (*five* pubs within a few yards of each other, all thriving). In St Just everything old seems to have been preserved including many of Cornwall's most ancient customs: St Just Feast Day, for instance, is the biggest and most renowned of any in the district.

Just as Land's End and other remote spots like Trencrom reflect the wilder and most romantic side of the area, so in a curious way St Just (and nearby Pendeen and Trewellard) could be said to mirror the human side of the ancient Cornish people. At St Just, for instance, along the road to Pendeen, you can still see the tall lifting wheels and chimneys of Geevor, one of the few surviving mines still operating in Cornwall – and immediately one is made conscious of still being in a part of the world where life goes on underground as well as on the surface. Somehow this seems a very important aspect of any understanding of what is meant by the term 'the Land's End Peninsula'.

So much for the scene: a misty and shadowy world pervaded with ghosts of the past, beauties of the present, intimations of the future. Enter it at your peril, Walter de la Mare would probably have said, but take comfort from the knowledge that you have had many illustrious predecessors, some of them among the most famous names in English literature. And so, read on.

II

Early Literary Travellers

Among the earliest travellers to write about West Cornwall was John Leland, the antiquary. In fact Leland spent the years 1534-43 travelling all over England, at some stage reaching down to the very end of the land itself – an experience that some 450 years later makes striking reading for a modern generation used to a rather changed landscape. Here, for instance, in his own wording of the time, is Leland's reflections of 'St Jes', or St Ives:

St Jes is two miles or more from Lannant. The Place that the chief of the Toun hath and partly dooth stande yn is a very Peninsula, and is extendid into the Sea of Severn as a Cape. Most Part of the Houses in the Peninsula be sore oppressid or overcoverid with Sandes that the stormy Windes and Rages castith up ther; this Calamite hath continuid ther little above 20 yeres. The best part of the Toun now standith in the South Part of the Peninsula, up towards another Hille, for Defence from the Sandes. There is a Blok House and a fair Pere in the Est side of the Peninsula, but the Pere is sore chokid with Sande. The Poroch Chirch is of Ja, a noble Man's Daughter of Ireland and Disciple of S Barricus. Ja and Elwine with many others cam into Cornewaul and landid at Pendinas. This Pendinas is the Peninsula and stony rock wher now the Toun of S Jes standith. One Dinan, a Great Lord in Cornewaul, made a Chirch at Pendinas at the Request of Ja, as it is written yn S Jes Legende. Ther is now at the very point of Pendinas a Chapel of S Nicolas and a Pharos for Lighte for Shippes sailing by Night in those Quarters. The Town of S Jes is servid with fresch water of Brokettes that rize in the Hilles therby.

More than a century after Leland the doughty Celia Fiennes, author of *Through England on a Side Saddle*, made an equally exhaustive study of this strange and distant county, describing her horse ride from Redruth to Land's End mostly over heath and downs which were very bleak and full of mines. Like so many of these early travellers, Celia Fiennes seems to have been fascinated not so much with scenery as with local customs and early signs of industrial developments such as the copper mines – 'the ore is something as the tin, only this looks blackish, or rather a purple colour and the glistering part is yellow as the other is white'.

She visited St Ives where the people carried all their things on horses' backs so that on a market day which was a Friday she saw a great number of horses little of size called Cornish *canelys*. At 'Pensands', a little market town that looked snug and warm, she noted that there was no wood or coal to spare and her supper at the cottage where she rested was boiling on a fire always supplied with a bush of furze. The way onwards to Land's End she found rather deserted and like the Peak country in Derbyshire, dry stone walls and hills full of stones, but in most places better land and yielding good corn, wheat, barley and oats and rye.

About two miles from Land's End she came in sight of the main ocean on both sides, the south and the north sea, and after reaching the point saw the 'island of Sily, which is 7 leagues off the Land's End.' She was told on a clear day those in the island could discern the people on the mainland as they went up the hill to church and they could even describe their clothes. The houses were poor cottages rather like barns, much like those in Scotland, but the insides were clean and plastered; for curiosity's sake she accepted a drink there and discovered very good bottled ale.

For these and a dozen other interesting mundane details Celia Fiennes' account is especially valuable as a social

document, but even her matter of fact observation raises its
level somewhat when standing at Land's End itself:

> So I went up pretty high hills and over some heath and
> common on which a great storm of hail and rain met me and
> drove fiercely on me but the wind soon dried my dust coat
> ... The Land's End terminates in a peak of great rocks
> which runs a good way into the sea. I clambered over them
> as far as safety permitted me. There are abundance of rocks
> and shoals of stones stand up in the sea a mile off, some
> here and there, some quite to the shore, which they name
> by several names of Knights and Ladies rolled up in
> mantles from some old tradition or fiction. The poets
> advance descriptions of the amours of some great persons:
> but these many rocks and stones, which look like the Needes
> on the Isle of Wight, make it hazardous for ships to double
> the point, especially in stormy weather.

However it is not long before, having returned inland towards
Hayle, our intrepid traveller is once again back to more
mundane observations about the bleakness and how the winds
are so troublesome that local people are forced to spin straw
and so to make a caul or network to lay over their thatch on
their ricks and outhouses with weights of stones around to
defend the thatch from being blown away by great winds.

Hayle, incidentally, also featured prominently in
Observations of the Western Counties by W.G. Maton, written
about 1794-6, in which he expressed horror at the conditions
in the smelting houses and the shocking appearance of the
workers. He described as dreadfully deleterious the fumes of
arsenic constantly impregnating the air of these places, and
noted that perspiration occasioned by the heat of the furnaces
was so profuse that those who had been employed at them but
a few months became most emaciated figures and in the
course of a few years were generally laid in their graves. Like
Leland and many other of these earlier travellers, Maton
seemed obsessively struck with the way the whole of the north-
western coast of Cornwall was constantly threatened by sands

– St Ives harbour choked with sand brought by north-west winds and the country around Hayle entirely covered with sand blown about by every blast of the wind, rendering its appearance truly dismal. All this, of course, fits in well as evidence or encouragement for the many famous Cornish legends of churches and villages buried under the sands.

Fortunately we are not totally dependent upon such worthy but rather pedestrian records: once the existence of this strange and romantic place became known, rather more distinguished literary figures were drawn westwards. Some, like Thomas Hardy, only got so far as Boscastle on the upper part of the north coast of Cornwall where the settings, however, are very similar to those of the Land's End area – a common imagery can be found in many of the marvellous poems which Hardy produced during his year's stay, poems that contain such captivating lines as 'When I set out for Lyonesse a hundred miles away' and 'O the opal and the sapphire of that wandering western sea', and again 'And the Atlantic dyed its levels with a dull misfeatured stain and then the sun burst out again and purples prinked the main'. Hardy was in fact forever looking westwards and returns continually to this kind of imagery: 'In chasmal beauty looms that wild weird western shore'.

Although he never spent much time down at Land's End itself Hardy was profoundly influenced by the whole melodramatic nature and appearance of the North Cornish coast. Certainly he regarded his year at Boscastle as one of the most significant in his whole life – as it was, of course, since he married the rector's daughter, Emma!

Most of the other visiting writers, unlike Hardy, were irresistibly drawn further towards the setting sun – 'where headland after headland flamed far into the rich heart of the west' to quote from the Poet Laureate himself, Alfred Lord Tennyson. It was in September 1860 that Tennyson embarked on a mammoth walking tour of Devon and Cornwall, accompanied by his fellow poet and editor of *The Golden Treasury* anthology, Francis Palgrave, together with two well-known painters of the day, Holman Hunt and Valentine

Prinsep. Fortunately for posterity, Tennyson kept a diary in which he claimed among other things that he often walked ten miles a day – though he admitted getting very tired of constantly beating in the face of the Cornish wind and rain. Nevertheless the tour obviously made deep impressions on Tennyson. He had already written the first four *Idylls of the King* but was still immersed in the great Arthurian legends so he was delighted to be back in Cornwall with its 'black cliffs and caves and storm and wind', all the elemental background he most desired. He loved the sea, and was especially pleased when finally the party reached the furthermost point of their journey and stayed at the Land's End Inn (presumably now 'The First and Last Inn').

Naturally the others made their notes, too, and we have an amusing comment by Holman Hunt about his august literary companion as 'in his slouch hat, his rusty black suit and his clinging coat, he wandered away among the rocks assiduously attended by our literary friend (Palgrave) and if by chance the poet escaped his eyes for a minute the voice of Palgrave was heard above the sea and the wind calling "Tennyson! Tennyson!"' Apparently this habit irritated Tennyson but as he detested publicity he would meekly allow himself to be caught up with rather than risk making himself the centre of attraction to locals and visitors.

Holman Hunt wrote on another occasion:

We painters placed ourselves upon a tongue of cliff which divided a large bight into smaller bays; thence we could, to right and left, see down to the emerald waves breaking with foam white as snow on the porphyry rocks. Tennyson had made up his mind to look down into the gulf and we had to find an abutting crag over which he could lean and survey the scene ... 'I could have stayed there all day,' said Tennyson.

Throughout the tour Tennyson's agile mind was taking in the richness of his surroundings and one finds him constantly noting down images – how the light fading through the

opening of a cave had a 'Rembrandt-like quality', or that
there was a 'Bewick-like look' about his trunk, cloak and bag
lying on a rock. He also observed that sculpture was
particularly good for the mind; there was a height and divine
stillness about it which preached peace to stormy passions. It
was from experiences like these, wandering over the great
desolate Cornish cliffs, that Tennyson was to evolve his
marvellous poetic imagery; 'The bare black cliffs clang'd
round him, as he based his feet on juts of slippery crag that
rang sharp-smitten with the dint of armed heels' – and again,
'The tide that sweeps above their coffined bones' and 'All
down the lonely coast of Lyonesse, Each with a beacon star
upon his head'. Oh, yes indeed, Alfred Lord Tennyson was
very much at home at the Land's End of 'glorious grass-green
monsters of waves'.

As might be expected there were lighter sides to the four
men's holiday walk. Towards the end of the trip the poets took
to travelling by dog-cart while the two painters walked. As
ever, Palgrave remained close to Tennyson who said he did
not want to spoil their holiday but in fact whenever he thought
he had found a quiet place in which to compose a few stanzas
he would hear 'Palgrave's voice like a bee in a bottle making
the neighbourhood resound with his name'. The next morning
Tennyson was up early hoping to be away – only to find
Palgrave joining him at the last moment.

It was a long and eventful tour. After leaving Land's End
the group went round the Lizard and then to Falmouth where
Tennyson met Caroline Fox, a noted Cornish literary lady
whose journals abound with accounts of intellectual
gatherings at her house, Penjerrick, with Carlyle, Kilvert, J.A.
Froude and many others of Tennyson's world. In her *Journal*
Miss Fox described Tennyson as 'a grand specimen of a man
with a magnificent head set on his shoulders like the capital of
a mighty pillar. His hair is long and wavy and covers a
massive head. He wears a beard and a moustache, which one
begrudges, as hiding so much of that firm, forceful but finely
chiselled mouth'. She drew Tennyson's attention to a picture
of Queen Guinevere he could see in the Royal Falmouth

Polytechnic and he told her about his further plans for King
Arthur and the *Idylls*. Generally the diaries outline a happy
pattern of wild days' ramblings followed by convivial evenings
at some wayside inn, and there are rather delightful pictures
of those evenings, dinner over, the pipes and port out, and
lengthy discussion about art and poetry and literary topics in
general. Much of this discussion centred on the subject of
Palgrave's *Golden Treasury*, but otherwise he does not seem to
have been profoundly influenced by his tour. Perhaps he was
too busy anxiously guarding the well-being of his older poet
friend.

Tennyson and Palgrave were not the only famous poets of
the nineteenth century to be drawn irresistibly to Land's End.
Algernon Swinburne, for instance, one of the Pre-Raphaelite
group, spent a major part of his poetic career working on the
one great legendary story associated forever with that region,
the tale of Tristan and Isolde. Other poets have tackled this
theme, including Tennyson, but there are many critics who
regard Swinburne's version, *Tristram of Lyonesse*, as the
greatest. Swinburne was a frequent visitor to Cornwall, and in
particular to the wild north coast regions, and one could quote
almost endlessly from his remarkable verse play.

And on the sounding soft funereal shore
They, watching till the days should wholly die,
Saw the far sea sweep to the far grey sky,
Saw the long sands sweep to the long grey sea.
And night made one sweet mist of moor and lea,
And only far off shore the foam gave light,
And life in them sank silent as the night.

And then again:

For the strong sea hath swallowed wall and tower,
And where their limbs were laid in woeful hour
For many a fathom gleams and moves and moans
The tide that sweeps above their coffined bones
In the wrecked chancel by the shivered shrine:

Nor where they sleep shall moon or sunlight shine
Nor man look down for ever: none shall say,
Here once, or here, Tristram and Iseult lay:
But peace they have that none may gain who live,
And rest about them that no love can give,
And over them, while death and life shall be,
The light and sound and darkness of the sea.

Before Tennyson's lively walking tour, two other eminent literary figures of the same period also came down to Cornwall: Charles Dickens, the novelist, and John Forster, the critic. The year was 1842, Dickens was just thirty years old and lately returned from a triumphant lecture tour of America. After entertaining the American poet Longfellow and seeing him off from Bristol on his return journey, Dickens agreed that it was time he had a holiday – so off he went with Forster, later to be his biographer, and two painters, Daniel Maclise and Clarkson Stanfield.

In many ways the tour sounds very like the later one by the Poet Laureate: a group of friends walking and talking, laughing and imbibing, staying in little inns and sitting up late into the night. Like Tennyson, Dickens had at the back of his mind combining business with pleasure by gathering material for a new novel he planned set 'in some terribly iron-bound spot on the Cornish coast'. Unlike Tennyson he kept no journal of his journey but his mood was well expressed in letters to friends.

Blessed star of morning, such a trip we had into Cornwall, just after Longfellow went away! We went down to Devonshire by railroad and there we hired an open carriage from an inn-keeper patriotic in all Pickwick matters and went on with post horses. Sometimes we travelled by night, sometimes all day, sometimes both. I kept the joint-stock purse, ordered all the dinners, paid all the turn-pikes and conducted facetious conversations with the post-boys and regulated the pace at which we travelled.

If you could have followed us into the earthy old

churches, and into the strange caverns of the gloomy
seashore and down into the depths of mines and up to the
top of giddy heights where unspeakable green water was
roaring. If you could have seen but one gleam of the bright
fires by which we sat in the big rooms of ancient inns at
night, until long after the small hours had come and gone,
or smelt but one steam of the hot punch, which came in
every evening in a huge broad china bowl. I never laughed
so much in my life as I did on this journey. Seriously I do
believe there never was such a trip. And they made such
sketches, these two men, in the most romantic of our
halting places that you would have sworn we had the Spirit
of Beauty with us, as well as the Spirit of Fun.

Forster, too, had some interesting things to say about the trip
during which he claims that no part of mountain or sea
consecrated to the legends of Arthur was left unexplored. He
describes the travellers climbing up to the highest tower of St
Michael's Mount in Mount's Bay, and they also visited some
of the West Cornwall mines. Forster does not leave any record
about the mines, but he has a vivid memory of Land's End
and – in the quotation I have already given in full in Chapter I
– how they all marvelled at the sinking of the sun behind the
Atlantic, 'a source of such deep emotion to us all'.
   Despite Dickens' literary plans, and his undoubted good
impressions of the Cornish scenery, he did not in the end set
his new novel (which turned out to be *Martin Chuzzlewit*) in
Cornwall, but in Wiltshire. However, Cornwall was by no
means forgotten, and nearly two decades later Dickens was
back again on yet another tour. This time his companion was
another famous writer of the day, the novelist Wilkie Collins,
then just putting the last touches to what was to be his most
successful book, *The Woman in White*. Collins describes how
the travellers were stared at with almost incredible pertinacity
and good humour by groups who congregated at cottage
doors.
   Some years earlier Collins had made a previous literary tour
of Cornwall during which, as he recounts in *Rambles Beyond*

Railways, he tramped from Land's End right along the north coast to Tintagel. These were the years when pilchard fishing was in its heyday, and while in St Ives Collins saw two and a half million fish caught in the big seine nets. One of the most interesting of his adventures was a descent of the Botallack Mine, near Pendeen, one of those mines so close to the sea that several galleries run out for a mile below the sea's surface. To reach these lower levels the miners had to descend as much as a thousand feet. Wilkie Collins went down too:

> The process of getting down the ladders was not very pleasant. They were all quite perpendicular, the rounds were placed at irregular distances, many of them were much worn away, and were slippery with water and copper ooze. Added to this, the narrowness of the shaft, the dripping wet rock shutting you in, as it were, all round your back and sides against the ladder – the fathomless darkness beneath it – the light flaring immediately above you as if your head was on fire – the voice of the miners below rumbling away in dull echoes lower and lower into the bowels of the earth – the consciousness that if the rungs of the ladder broke you might fall down a thousand feet or so of narrow tunnel in a moment – imagine all this and you may easily realise what are the first impressions produced by a descent into a Cornish mine.

Further along the north coast Collins came upon a grim reminder of what really faces those whose lives are spent 'at peril at sea' when he visited an old churchyard.

> Within the churchyard the bright colour of the turf and the grey houses of the mouldering tombstones are picturesquely intermingled all over the uneven surface of the ground, save in one remote corner where the graves are few and the grass grown rank and high. Here the eye is abruptly attracted to the stern of a boat, painted white and fixed upright in the earth. This strange memorial, little suited though it be to the old monuments around, has a

significance of its own which gives it peculiar claim to consideration.

Inscribed on it appeared the names of ten fishermen of the parish who went out to sea to pursue their calling on one wintry night in 1846. It was unusually cold on land – on the sea the frosty, bitter wind cut through the bones. The men were badly provided against the weather; and hardy as they were, the weather killed them that night. In the morning, the boat drifted to shore, manned like a spectre bark by the ghastly figures of the dead – freighted horribly with the corpses of all ten men frozen to death. They now lie buried in the churchyard and the stern of the boat they died in tells their fatal story and points to the last home which they share together.

The Reverend Robert Francis Kilvert, regarded as one of England's most entertaining diarists, was another visitor to Cornwall, actually in the same year as Thomas Hardy (1870). He went to stay with some old friends, the Hockins, who lived at Perranarworthal, near Truro, and from there he paid numerous journeys down to the magical world of Land's End and Lyonesse. He does not seem to have been greatly impressed by his first sight of Cornwall, describing it as bleak, barren and uninteresting and noting that the most striking features appeared to be the innumerable mine works of lead, tin and copper which crowned the hills with tall chimney shafts and ugly, white, dreary buildings, or alternatively could be found nestling in some deep, narrow valley defiling and poisoning the streams with the white tin washing. Later, however, delighted by the sight of purple heather on the cliffs and the beautiful shrub and camelias of his hostess's semi-tropical garden, Kilvert became more enthusiastic.

The Cornish seem to be a fine tall folk, especially the women, much taller, larger people than the Welsh, and most of them appear to be dark haired. They are very kind and neighbourly to each other especially when they are in trouble ... The Penzance people and especially the women are said to be the handsomest in Cornwall.

Reading *Kilvert's Diary* covering that holiday, one gets a delightful picture of a gay social life with constant family outings in horse-drawn wagonnettes, usually accompanied by a large picnic basket and liberal quantities of sherry – though by all accounts frequent stops were also made at wayside inns. This was notably so on the day of a memorable outing to Land's End when the party called at Treen Inn, near the Logan Rock, to drink ale and cider, and subsequently took their hamper indoors and had a capital dinner at the Gurnard's Head Hotel.

At Gurnard's Head Kilvert seems to have enjoyed one of his most memorable times in Cornwall, being able to wander off alone among the rocks at the furthest point and there to 'sit alone amongst the wilderness of broken shattered tumbled cliffs listening to the booming and breaking of the waves below and watch the flying skirts of the showers of spray.' At the request of Mrs Hockin who wanted specimens of a special sea fern which grows in the rocks, Kilvert went clambering all over the steep-sided cliffs and finally found the requisite fern, with its 'bright glossy green leaves'. Then it was on the road again for a long ride to Rosewarne, for dinner at midnight with some friends, finally arriving back at the Hockins' house at three in the morning – having set out the previous day at 9 a.m.

Altogether Kilvert covered an enormous area of West Cornwall during his stay, visiting St Michael's Mount, Penzance, Zennor, St Ives, and many other beauty spots. Possibly he was most intrigued by 'the last happy day' when the whole party went off to that strange place, Gwithian, on the edge of St Ives Bay, to look at the ancient buried church whose remains had been dug out from the sands only a few years before. These remains had been identified as those of one of the earliest Christian buildings in Britain built at least a hundred years before St Augustine came to Britain, so, as a clergyman, Kilvert was very moved.

We came to the place suddenly and without warning and looked down into the church as into a long pit. The sand is drifted solid up to the very top of the outside walls. The walls are about four feet high measured from the inside. So far they are almost perfect. The material is granite with a good deal of pure felspar, of which I brought away a pretty pink piece. The church is quite a small building, oblong, a door and window place still perceptible and the faint remains of the rude pillars of a chancel arch still to be made out. Within the memory of persons still living the altar was standing but the place has got into the hands of a dissenting farmer who keeps the place for a cattle yard and sheep fold – what more need be said. I wish that some people of influence in the neighbourhood would bestir themselves and rescue from utter destruction and oblivion this most interesting relic of earliest British Christianity.

Kilvert seems to have been fascinated by Gwithian, 'this village by the sea', and crossed the sand-dunes to take a look at Godrevy lighthouse. He mentions in his diary that a former curate of the district had been drowned while exercising his dog on the beach and that a window in the church commemorated him – a fact that came back when some months later he had a disturbing dream that he, Kilvert, was living as a curate at Gwithian! It was at Gwithian, in effect, that Kilvert as he put it in his diary, took a last longing, hungering farewell look at the Cornish sea, and it was of the sea, again, that he thought when finally he embarked on his railway journey back to England.

A bitter moment it was when the Tamar was crossed and Cornwall left behind, perhaps for ever. I seemed to linger once more over the last fond look at the Cornish sea. And in what company. I thought – was it so – that there were tears in those blue eyes when we parted. I know there were tears in mine. Forget me not, oh, forget me not.

We have no record either of who was the owner of this particular pair of blue eyes or of any return to Cornwall by the Reverend Kilvert, but it is interesting to observe how three weeks spent mostly in the magical far west of the country left such a profound impression upon the diarist.

George Borrow may seem an unlikely author to have Cornish connections, but in fact *Lavengro* opens with these words: 'My father was a Cornishman, the youngest, as I have heard him say, of seven brothers; he sprang from a family of gentlemen, or, as some people would call them, *gentillantres*, for they were not wealthy; they had a coat of arms, however, and lived on their own property, at a place called Tredinnock which, being interpreted, means the house on the hill, which house and the neighbouring acres had been from time immemorial in their possession.' Borrow's father seems to have been as strong and determined a character as his son, for he won fame as a Cornish wrestler and even travelled to London for a contest in Hyde Park where he fought a drawn battle with Big Ben Brain.

Borrow's father came from St Cleer, near Liskeard, but being a soldier he was stationed all over the country and George was actually born in Norfolk. In fact he never saw Cornwall for half a century, by which time he was quite famous – his *Bible of Spain* had run into six editions in its first year of publication. No doubt intrigued by all the publicity some of the Cornish members of his family wrote begging the pleasure of a visit from their renowned cousin. True to his favourite style when George Borrow finally entered the 'land of his forefathers' he did so as part of one of his usual 'tramps', in this case heading – where else? – for Land's End. On the way he called in to meet his relatives at Penquite Farm, St Cleer, where in fact he spent a Christmas Day, (and went off with alacrity to inspect the Trevethy Domen holed-stone, believed to have superstitious powers – without ado thrusting his arm through the hole and crying out, 'Success to Old Cornwall!').

The real old Cornwall for Borrow was obviously more likely to be found at the end of that long, rambling county and in the early days of the new year of 1854 we find him setting off from St Cleer – in the words of his cousin, Mrs Taylor, 'a fine tall man of about six feet three, well proportioned, and not stout, able to walk five miles an hour successively ... the more I see of

him the less I know of him.' After pausing at Redruth to
ascend the huge granite sentinel of Carn Brea, where he noted
that the large basin must have been a horrid place of sacrifice
judging by the outlets for the blood to stream down, Borrow
walked in a single day the twenty miles or so to Mousehole.
He was especially interested by the traces of Spanish and
gypsy descent on this part of the coast, and was also drawn to
visit the grave at Paul Church of Dolly Pentreath, the last
person to speak native Cornish. After that Borrow wandered
on with increased delight along the tempestuous southern
coast, visiting Lamorna and Penberth and especially walking
out to Treryn to see the Logan Rock. Apparently while out
there he fell into conversation with an Irish tinker from whom
he heard strange gypsy tales – an experience woven into
Romany Rye.

Altogether Borrow spent six weeks in Cornwall, much of the
time in Penwith country and as ever he was quick to pick up
useful tales of local folklore. He noted that everywhere in
Cornwall there was still a firm belief in the pixies, quoting one
of his cousins as having heard the 'durdy dogs', or 'dandy
dogs', who were supposed to dash over moorlands and other
desolate places led by demon huntsmen chasing the souls of
the wicked – it was perilous to hear them and even more
perilous to hail them. Although by that time an accomplished
linguist from his many travels it seems that Borrow found
considerable difficulty in understanding the Cornish dialect.
'You can only see Cornwall or know anything about it by
walking through it – it is romantic to a degree, though
probably one would not like to live in it.'

Borrow left Cornwall in order to visit the British Museum
and start collecting material for his forthcoming *Romany Rye*.
He never went back – and yet obviously Cornwall left quite an
impression on his agile imagination for when *Romany Rye*
finally appeared it contained a large advertisement of 'a
forthcoming book on Cornwall'. As in the case of Dickens, the
intention proved firmer than any final resolve and no Cornish
book ever appeared. This seems a great pity for though
Borrow was notoriously slapdash on facts any man who could

produce such vivid word pictures as are to be found in *Lavengro* or *Wild Wales* would surely have touched on a few profound truths about Cornwall and all its mysteries. While down near Land's End, for instance, he met several Romany families and was able to converse with them in their own tongue, and it would have been fascinating to have made a record of that side of local life.

Although not exactly a literary figure, the great painter J.M.W. Turner may surely be allowed to intrude here, for when he was thirty-six years old and at the height of his burgeoning powers as a painter he also made an extensive tour of Cornwall – from which emerged many of his most famous paintings, such as 'Longships Lighthouse', 'Land's End', 'St Mawes at the Pilchard Season', 'East and West Looe', and 'The Lost Sailor or Storm over the Lizard'. Turner was nothing if not the perfectionist in his approach to capturing the true drama and feeling of Cornwall, and his friend Cyrus Redding, a writer who accompanied him on some of the trip, has described in some awe how at times Turner would go to such extremes as having himself lashed to the mast of a boat so that he could observe a storm at sea without being washed overboard.

During his Cornish tour Turner's paintings reflect the profound way he was influenced by the weather: storms, deluges, wrecks, blizzards, these were the sort of settings he revelled in – and of course he found them in plenty in Cornwall. For an artist so much in love with the sea and drama he could not have chosen a better setting – little wonder that he responded to it so marvellously. Of course he was a tough traveller and he would often walk twenty-five miles a day when young, and was used to sleeping rough. Redding describes how they stayed at one West Cornwall inn where there was no sleeping accommodation: after supping on bread and cheese and porter Turner began talking 'with a fluency I never heard before or after'. Sometimes in the early hours of the morning the painter simply leaned on the table and slept ... they were off again soon after dawn!

In a perceptive article contributed to the *Cornish Review* Ida

Proctor has given us this vivid image of Turner in Cornwall:

> Turner may have painted Cornwall larger than life,
> increasing the menace of huge waves and the steepness of
> cliff faces, as he exaggerated St Michael's Mount, making it
> rear up among the clouds in a revelation of light, with its
> castle perched on an enchanted pinnacle, but to an artist
> who had always loved the sea passionately, ever since his
> first sight of it in his Margate schooldays Cornwall offered
> him just what he needed: real life dramas in place of
> classical myths; rocks and wrecks, cliff castles and island
> homes, boats and fishermen at work; and a wide range of
> tones from softest spray and morning mists to stark rocks
> and blackest storm clouds. Turner was a short ungainly
> young man in his quaint ill-fitting clothes, slovenly in
> appearance, but undeterred by wind, rain, fog or gales,
> travelled the length of Cornwall by stagecoach or on foot,
> trudging along its rough roads, probably with his umbrella
> under his arm and certainly with his sketch book and pencil
> in his pocket, seeking the star turns of the Cornish
> landscape from the cliff edge, the beach, the quayside or the
> hilltop.
>
> Many remarked on his eccentricities but few who met
> him ever forgot the light in his grey blue eyes, which the son
> of artist C.R. Leslie said 'were those of a man long
> accustomed to looking straight at the face of nature through
> fair and foul weather alike'. Inspired by a thrilling
> admiration for the natural wonders of the world, he looked
> up to mountains and rocks, forest and fortresses, breaking
> waves and stormy heavens as a small man mentally
> cowering before their might and height, at the same time
> seemingly determined to make his audience tremble, too.

Turner's trip around Cornwall took him from mid-July to
mid-September, during which period he covered some 600
miles and made many hundreds of sketches. At least twenty
pictures of Cornish subjects were painted, either on the spot or
from sketches – some have since gone to America, others are in

museums here. None, surely, can rival for effect that dramatic study of the Longships Lighthouse of which Ruskin commented that it was as if the whole surface of the sea becomes one dizzy whirl of rushing, writhing, tortured undirected rage, bounding and crashing, and coiling in an anarchy of enormous power.

So much for the visitors. During this same period the Land's End area was nurturing writers of its own, particularly in the field of archaeology and antiquities, nature and the like. Many of these seemed to congregate around Penzance. A famous local literary figure in the district in the eighteenth century was the Rector of Ludgvan, Dr William Borlase, author of *Observations on the Antiquities of Cornwall, The Age of Saints*, and many other learned treatises on the county's history. The good doctor was quite a character: here is a portrait of him by a contemporary, General Walter Tremenheere;

I remember frequently seeing him at Castle Horneck. He used to drive a couple of bays, 'tandem', and was the only gentleman in that part of the country who ever did so. I remember his figure accurately, with his large wig and rather short stature. It was his habit, on his return from his morning drive to see his brother at Castle Horneck, to pull up at the only bookshop then in town, Hemming's, just above Mrs Trweeke's great house, and go in and see what books had been ordered by the families in the neighbourhood, and to read the papers, while his servant, who was always with him, held his horses.

Comfortable days! Mind you, prejudices were high, and not lacking in Dr Borlase who was affronted to hear of the impending arrival at St Just of the dastardly John Wesley – the people of St Just, he thundered, should have a due sense of the irregularity and ill-tendency of Mr Wesley's principles and practice because that unfortunate parish, being populous and containing few people of figure or knowledge, was one of 'this quack's' constant stages. Perhaps this indignation was partly because the good doctor had a particular fondness for the striking atmosphere around St Just, the bleak northern sea edged by steep and craggy hills and the hills and valleys equally bestrewed with rocks – although, alas, as he sourly observed, everywhere one met with mountains of rubbish thrown up out of tin mines. By contrast he once reflected more happily about his own home area:

I have had the pleasure of seeing some of the most considerable places in England, and I think there is hardly any place where I could so willingly wish that my lot had fallen as where it has. There is no part of England that abounds so much in the necessaries and at the same time has so many of the elegancies of life as that of Mount's Bay. The gentry, most of whom are our near relations, are of a free frolicking disposition. In the summer time we meet (some ten or a dozen) at a bowling green, there we have built a little pleasure house and there we dine, after dinner at bowls, and by so frequently meeting together we are as it were like so many brothers of one family, so united and so glad to see one the other. For my particular part since I have had the good fortune of a settlement it has required all my care and attention to get my habitation, which was a most ruinous one when I came to it, in some tolerable order. I have now, I thank God, made it somewhat comfortable and easy and to my great satisfaction not only made the house tenantable but from a wilderness or rather brake of briars and thorns have shaped out a little garden where I may have plenty one time or other, and where I have at present some pretty airy walks, thriving plantations, and clear running water; neither is my water barren cold or uninhabited, but there are fish in store which leap and play together in a pond I have and supply me with a little dish of excellent shots upon any emergent occasion. In my garden I spend most of my time outdoors, having not the good fortune to delight much in hunting or in shooting, diversions which I am forever far from finding fault with in others and for which our country is abundantly well provided.

At the period when Dr Borlase was writing Penzance was
becoming one of the cultural centres of Cornwall, noted in
particular for the strength of local archaeological interest. It
was around this time that one of the most fascinating books
ever written about Land's End made its appearance on the
bookstalls. This is J.T. Blight's *A Week at the Land's End*, issued
in 1861, which presented far and away the most detailed
introduction to a region which Blight claimed presented
scenes and memories which no other district in England
offered.

There are the bold, magnificent cliffs, and 'towering
headlands crowned with mist', guardians of the western
coast. There are hoary monuments of ages past – many of
them well preserved from the destroying hands of Time,
yet surrounded by a deep halo of mystery which the
speculations of the antiquary can scarcely penetrate. In
early days the rich merchants of Phoenicia made long
voyages hither, and in exchange for a few trinkets procured
the valuable metals of the soil. The Roman eagles here
contested with the warlike Cornish; and the sea kings, the
piratical Danes, made fell swoops wherever they could
effect a landing on the coast. It was here, too, that the
Saxons overthrew the army of Howel, the last of the
Cornish kings. Besides kings, princes, warriors, and
merchants, with all the train of romantic associations
connected with them, shadows of a deeper kind pass before
us, in the shape of long-robed Druids, the priests of Celtic
days – here they had their altars on the high hills and
cairns, here 'true to the awful rites of old' they paced the
vast circle's solemn round. Inscriptions and records they
have left none, for the deeds of this age were remembered
through the unwritten utterances of the Bard, and thus was
handed down the traditionary lore of a spot once occupied
by men whose religion and practices have forever vanished
away – the rough unhewn stone is the only visible landmark
of the peculiarities of their faith and worship.

That is a typical example of the erudite and entertaining style of Blight's book which he himself illustrated with nearly 100 engravings of ancient buildings, rocks, plants, birds and fishes. His industry was prodigious and he insisted on visiting every little cove and cairn in person:

> I have been out day after day amongst the rocks and furze, measuring and planning camps, hut circles, kistvaens and cromlechs. Got another cave partly dug into – shall finish it. All my sketches of these things, fairly finished and will be stuck in a good solid scrap book to come into somebody's hands after my departure. Be of value some day when the originals are all departed.

It should be remembered that Blight began his writing career at a time when Land's End still tended to be looked on as a country of its own. However there was then developing a strong element of local scholarship provided by such eminent figures as Dr Borlase, Davies Gilbert and Humphry Davy. Suddenly many more archaeologists and botanists and geologists began visiting the area. As John Michel has pointed out in his perceptive study *A Short Life by the Land's End*, to lovers of the picturesque Land's End had suddenly become an inviting prospect, a place of Druid memorials, of venerable altars and Logan rocks, with grand scenery, unique flora and mild bracing climate. With all these charming things located together in a remote country, hard by the legendary lost land of Lyonesse, Land's End became a magnetic centre of pilgrimage. Imaginative people suddenly began flocking there instigating a minor literary renaissance and a more considerable artistic one.

Perhaps these visitors helped to encourage the development of the Penzance Library, a unique institution still flourishing behind a fragrant magnolia tree in the Morrab Gardens – at which John Blight once occupied the position of assistant librarian. It was partly through the knowledge that he acquired at this library that Blight was encouraged to accumulate the notes for his first book, *Ancient Crosses and other Antiquities in the West of Cornwall*, describing and illustrating fifty-five stone crosses, five local cromlechs and sundry relics. It is interesting to find in the list of official subscribers such eminent local names as Borlase, Bolitho, Boase, le Grice, Couch, Cornish, Tonkin, as well as those of Sabine Baring Gould and R.S. Hawker. In due course both Hawker and the well-known antiquary, J.O. Halliwell, were to advise Blight on his career and help him where possible: through Halliwell, for instance, he received commissions to illustrate a number of volumes of antiquary interest. Aware of his own outstanding talents, particularly as an illustrator, Blight became extremely ambitious in the literary field envisaging such projects as a three-volume novel, commentaries on *Pilgrim's Progress*, books of religious verse, a new magazine to be called *The Archaeologist*.

Unfortunately, being a young man of exceptionally highly nervous temperament, John Blight eventually had a serious mental breakdown and for two years had to be looked after by his parents at their home in Morrab Place, Penzance. During this period he became frenzied and irrational, trying to keep on his literary work but unable to control his increasingly wild fantasies. In madness he became a fanatic, developing the idea that the ancient Druids had re-appeared and were plotting to restore their bloody rites as clergymen of the Church of England. He would even go about speaking on this theme, and took to writing half-crazed letters both to friends and to eminent figures such as Gladstone. At the same time he began work on what was to be his last book, *The Cromlechs of Cornwall*, a book that was never completed. Finally in 1871 Blight was committed to Bodmin Asylum, where he spent the rest of his days until he died in 1884.

As anyone who reads *A Week at the Land's End* will appreciate, the shortened career of J.F. Blight is a sad shadow in our study of Penwith. He was a man of prodigious talent, as is demonstrated in his engravings, and could well have surpassed such earlier figures as William Borlase, giving us a more detailed picture of Land's End and its history than has ever yet been provided (or ever now can be provided; one of Blight's firm if rather gloomy predictions was that many of the monuments and stones he so carefully recorded would not be left unmolested – and many have indeed already disappeared). A natural son of Penzance – in his last year of sanity he wrote that he was reconciled to living there and that nowhere else would he find such kind people, such peace and contentment – he fell between the two stools, on the one hand seeking national celebrity, and in so doing losing touch with his roots.

Perhaps one of the lesser known literary aspects of this same general period is also one of the most fascinating. Although quite rightly the literary fame of the Brontes is forever associated with Haworth on the bleak Yorkshire moors, it is worth remembering that their mother, Maria Branwell, was Cornish, third daughter of Mr Thomas Branwell, a merchant of Penzance (the mother's maiden name being the good old Cornish one of Carne). In 1812 Maria went on a visit to Yorkshire and while there she met the Reverend Patrick Bronte, at the time a curate at Hartshead near Dewbury: they fell in love and were married and in fact Maria never returned to Cornwall. Three years later they settled at Haworth when her husband became vicar there. In the space of eight years Maria gave birth to six children, two of whom died young. Undoubtedly this helped to weaken her health greatly and she died at the early age of thirty-eight, leaving her unhappy husband confronted with the task of rearing Emily, Charlotte, Anne and their brother Branwell. Fortunately for the Reverend Bronte, Maria's sister, Elizabeth, agreed to come up from Penzance and help look after the children and keep the home going. In Mrs Gaskell's *Life of Charlotte Bronte* there is this description of the Cornishwoman from Penzance who during the next few years inevitably had a profound influence on the Bronte sisters:

Miss Branwell was, I believe, a kindly and conscientious woman with a good deal of character, but with the somewhat narrow ideas natural to one who had spent nearly all her life in the same place. She had strong prejudices and soon took a distaste to Yorkshire. From

Penzance, where plants which we in the North call greenhouse flowers grow in great profusion and without any shelter even in the winter, and where the soft warm climate allows the inhabitants, if so disposed, to live pretty constantly in the open air, it was a great change for a lady considerably past forty to come and take up her abode in a place where neither flowers nor vegetables would flourish and where a tree of even moderate dimensions might be hunted for far and wide: where the snow lay long and late on the moors stretching bleakly and barely far up from the dwelling which was henceforth to be her home: and where often, on autumnal or winter nights, the four winds of heaven seemed to meet and rage together, tearing round the house as if they were wild beasts striving to find an entrance. She missed the small round of cheerful social visiting perpetually going on in a country town and she disliked many of the customs of the place and particularly dreaded the cold arising from the floors in the passages and parlours of Haworth Parsonage.

Miss Branwell appeared unaware of the fermentation of unoccupied talent going on around her, claimed Mrs Gaskell, but her judgement seems a little harsh, especially if we study the journal of Charlotte's friend Ellen Nussey. She gives a very different picture of Miss Branwell, dressing up gaily in silks – 'she very probably had been a belle among her acquaintances in her younger days' – and taking snuff out of a pretty little gold snuff box and enjoying the slight shock and astonishment this caused – above all, apparently spending long evenings reading aloud to Mr Bronte and then participating very animatedly in lively discussions on what they had been reading 'intelligent in her talk and tilting argument without fear against Mr Bronte'.

From this surely more accurate comment, and indeed similar ones that can be found by diligently searching among the writings of Charlotte and Emily, it would seem that the Branwell side of the family was an intellectual force to be reckoned with – so it would not seem unreasonable for

Penzance to claim a fair share in the eventual shaping of the fortunes of the Bronte sisters. For instance, although *Wuthering Heights* will always be associated with the Yorkshire moors, it should be remembered that Emily Bronte would have heard countless stories from her mother and her aunt about their own growing up surrounded by the wild moorlands of West Cornwall ... and there are many relics and stones up on the Penwith hills that would serve as models for Penistone Crags in Emily's famous novel. Then again those elements of ghostly hauntings so prevalent in *Wutherings Heights* may well have been encouraged in Emily's imaginations by countless stories told her as a child by her Cornish aunt, based on old Cornish legends. Certainly in the creation of her powerful masterpiece Emily must have drawn on an imagination partly bequeathed her from faraway Cornwall – and the same no doubt could he said for Charlotte, Anne and Branwell.

Penzance was the last home of one of the best known Victorian poets, a man whom T.S. Eliot once acknowledged as perhaps his greatest influence – writing of the poem 'Thirty Bob a Week' the personage created in this poem has haunted me all my life and the poem is to me a great poem forever'. His name was John Davidson, and he produced more than half a dozen collections of poetry, and several blank verse plays including one gigantic effort, *God and Mammon*, generally regarded as his major work. In his heyday Davidson was a contemporary of Yeats, Wilde, Shaw and Swinburne and other contributors to *The Yellow Book*, but later he became disillusioned, and it was this that led him in the last period of his life to retire to West Cornwall. He wrote only a little poetry while in Penzance – there is a nice poem describing St Michael's Mount as a 'piled elaborate flower of granite that the sun could not wither nor any tempest overthrow.' But perhaps one of his most fascinating pieces of writings from Cornwall took the form of a vivid reportage of a typical Cornish fair of that time.

It is by imagination that religion or any cause lives and prospers. If you doubt this of the Salvation Army, attend its meetings. You can do so with me, now, at the Land's End. It is the annual carnival in West Penwith. The town stands on a slope, and the Fair Ground is behind on the top of the hill. At the entrance to the Fair the Salvation Army occupies a stance every night like a lion in the path; but nobody is scared, and with few exceptions none pay any heed ... It is an extensive Fair. The further from London the bigger the fair. When there is no music hall within a hundred miles of the town all the showmen in England may cut and come again. On the clouded sky at night the ruddy oil lamps of the stalls and the pale electric lights of the merry go rounds and the theatres spread a mixed lacquer of tarnished gold, dusky emerald and swarthy purples visible from all parts of the town, and for miles around, alluring the fancy of the young and the old, a convincing sign in the heavens of entertainment, frolic and festivity ... For three days and three nights this travelling suburb of frivolity is thronged by Cornish crowds from all the towns, villages and farms in the neighbourhood. All classes are represented, all ages, with one mood, with one will in all – the intention to be happy.

Of one thing all the frequenters of the Fair are certain, on each visit at least, that happiness is possible here below; and they are all bent on one more bid for it, seeing that their carnival has come round again. What they enjoy is a satisfied imagination. The bioscope and the merry go rounds, the flaring and dazzling lights, the tumult of the music, and the uproar of the crowd over-brim the imagination of the frequenter of the Fair. He has only to walk up the hill to be filled with light and colour, sound and movement, to have his imagination clothed as with a Universe of suns and systems. At the gate of the Fair stands religion, preferring to the ephemeral vanities of the travelling showman a vision of the Universe itself; but the vision is not patent, and the Fair is; and so the pleasure seeker passes in ...

Obviously a writer of great talent, Davidson longed to write a great poem which expressed his Lucretian Materialism. Learning of this one of his admirers, Bernard Shaw, sent down £250 to enable him to get on with his proposed masterpiece. Unfortunately the effort must have proved too much mentally, and already full of a deep despair –

> Farewell the hope that mocked, farewell despair
>   That went before me still, and made the pace.
> The earth is full of graves, and mine was there
>   Before my life began, my resting-place;
> And I shall find it out and with the dead
>   Lie down for ever all my sayings said. –

Davidson considered that the time had arrived to fulfil what he had already declared to be man's unchallengeable privilege. On the last day of his life, sitting in his Penzance cottage, he wrote the preface to his final book of poems and posted the manuscript to his publisher, Grant Richard. When the parcel was opened in London it contained this message:

> The time has come to make an end. There are several motives. I find my pension is not enough; I have therefore still to turn aside and attempt things for which people will pay. My health also counts. Asthma and other annoyances I have tolerated for years; but I cannot put up with cancer ...

Davidson then went out and drowned himself in the waters of Mount's Bay; his body finally washed up near Mousehole.

W.H. Hudson, born 1841, is another writer principally of the Victorian period, who towards the end of his life became strongly associated with the Land's End area. It was about the turn of the century in fact when, in the hope of finding some relief from a weak heart and endless bronchial troubles and rheumatism he journeyed for the first time down to Cornwall, renting lodgings in the Terrace, St Ives, overlooking the harbour. He was at once delighted with the climate, especially the days when the sky was clear, the wind still and the sun flooded the world with light and heat. Such days, he reflected, were apt to be warmer than in other parts; even the adder, hibernating in his deep dark den beneath the rock, was stirred by the heavenly influence and crawled forth on a mid winter day to lie basking in the delicious beams. The entire visible world, sea and land seemed like a glittering serpent, its discontent now forgotten, slumbering peacefully, albeit with wide open eyes, in the face of the sun ...

From the beginning Hudson was fascinated by the wild, hilly moorland in Penwith, walking for hours along cliff tops or forcing his way over rocky barriers and through thickets of furze to inspect inland areas. Soon he had accumulated such a pile of nature notes that he began writing articles for magazines, and from these, ultimately, developed one of his most famous books, *The Land's End: A Naturalist's Impressions in West Cornwall*, issued 1908. This was in fact much more than merely rural impressions: Hudson wrote with equal perception about the Cornish people and their manners, morals and other characteristics. He hated the local practices of trapping wild birds on fish hooks or in steel gins and revealed with disgust how in some treeless place where birds crowded into bushes to roost at night whole gangs equipped with lanterns and armed with sticks were going out and beating the area and killing the birds. At the same time he wrote vividly about the more mystical side of life at Land's End. In particular he seemed extremely receptive to thoughts of the ancient dead which came to him, as once when he sat on an old burial mound:

They were there with me in the twilight on the barrow in crowds, sitting and standing in groups, and many lying on their sides on the turf below, their heads resting in their hands ... Evening by evening for many and many a century they had looked to that point, towards the horizon where there were people and sounds of human life ... looked with apprehension since men still dwell, strangers to them, little busy eager people, hateful in their artificial indoor lives, who do not know and who care nothing for them, who worship not and fear not the dead that are underground but dig up their sacred places and scatter their bones and ashes, and despise and mock them because they are dead and powerless.

It is not strange that they fear and hate. I look at them – their dark, pale, furious faces – and think that if they could be visible thus in the daylight, all who came to that spot or passed near it would turn and fly with a terrifying image in their mind which would last to the end of life. But they do not resent my presence, and would not resent it were I permitted to come at last to dwell with them for ever. Perhaps they know me for one of their tribe – know that what they feel I feel, would hate what they hate.

What a powerful writer – and how natural that he should be so drawn to the Land's End area. In fact for the last decade of his life Hudson settled into a routine whereby he left London every November and stayed down in Cornwall until the following May or June. His search for suitable winter quarters took him to Lelant, Flushing, Looe and Fowey, but at last he settled for comfortable lodgings in rooms facing south in Penzance. On previous visits he had not paid the town much attention, but now over the years he grew to like it greatly and became a well-known local figure – for instance at the Morrab Library, in the lovely semi-tropical gardens, where he had easy access to the works of other great naturalists in the marvellous collection of 10,000 books there.

During his last years in Cornwall Hudson continued writing vigorously, and indeed during that period produced what has been described as one of the most extraordinary autobiographies ever written, *Far Away and Long Ago*, the story of his childhood in a distant country written by a man in his seventy-fourth year. When he sent the manuscript to Edward Garnett, the literary critic and publisher's reader, Garnett said it was a masterpiece, and when it was published it was widely acclaimed. Financially perhaps his most successful book was the novel *Green Mansions*, ten thousand copies of which were sold in the first year of publication, and which by the time of Hudson's death had been reprinted nearly twenty times. As a writer he was always conscientious and penetrating and West Cornwall has good reason to be proud of such a literary son, even if an adopted one. Somehow it seems a fitting epitaph that after his death a group of local Cornishmen took the trouble to inscribe on a rock on top of one of his favourite hills at Zennor: *W.H. Hudson Often Came Here.*

Zennor and the surrounding area was also at one time familiar country to a group of local writers of a rather different kind. It used to be the fashion in the older days for Cornwall to be travelled by wandering balladeers or *droll* tellers who composed songs and poems in the traditional style and earned their living by such old crafts as knife-grinding, peg-selling and stone-cutting. These balladeers would wander from one village to the next always sure of a welcome, including a meal and a bed, in return for a nominal 'rent' of a song or a story. One of the best known of these balladeers came from the small village of Sancreed, just off the road from Penzance to Land's End. His name was Billy Foss and many of his verses and rhymes were passed round from hand to hand written down on scraps of paper. They were almost invariably rather malicious, like this description of a local farm:

> As I traversed Boslow I saw an old cow,
> A hog and a flock of starved sheep,
> Besides an old mare, whose bones were so bare
> As to make its poor master to weep.

There are several more verses in the same vein. Billy Foss was also rather fond of brief epitaphs: 'Beneath this stone lies a rotten body, the mortal remains of Betty Toddy' and 'The rogues and thieves in Buryan Town, they stole the sheaves and the mow fell down.'

Henry Quick of Zennor was equally known in the area and it is still possible to find his old broadsheets in some Penwith farms. He appears to have been a more talented writer than Billy Foss, if perhaps lacking the latter's pungent malice. For most of his life he lived with his mother and when she died in 1843 he described himself as struggling on like a water wheel that had no stream. However, before he himself died in 1858 he penned this epitaph:

> The Cornish drolls are dead, each one;
> The fairies from their haunts have gone.
> There's scarce a witch in all the land,
> The world has grown so learn'd and grand.

By and large it would seem that in Land's End the eighteenth and nineteenth centuries produced a combination, as I have shown, of excited and stimulated visiting writers and of a smaller group of studious and conscientious workers who were either born in the district, like Borlase or Davy, or settled there, like Hudson. Looking back, apart from these I have briefly touched upon, one should not forget, in passing, a whole group of eccentric figures such as R.S. Hawker, the vicar of Morwenstow, famous not merely for his poetry and works, such as *Footprints of Former Men in Far Cornwall*, but also for practical jokes, like dressing up as a mermaid and being towed along the seashore – or his fellow cleric, Sabine Baring Gould who, though based at Lewdon in Devon, made numerous forays into Cornwall and Land's End in particular (using the area as a setting for several of his thirty novels, one of the best known being *In the Roar of the Sea*).

John Harris, the miner poet of Camborne, also comes to mind: a strangely neglected figure, somewhat resurrected thanks to the loving attention of a contemporary Cornish poet, D.M. Thomas. Harris's work is full of imagery that might almost have been hammered into him by the Cornish landscape.

> How the great mountain like a rocky king
> Stands silent in the tempest! Not a gust
> With water laden, rushing with fierce front
> Against his wrinkles, but he shakes it off,
> Like filmy atoms from an insect's wing.

The thunder growls upon his splinter'd head,
Yelling from cave to cave and every crag,
Carved by the Druid in the olden time,
When men were went to worship on his crest,
Seems like a fiery pillar, as the flames
Leap from the clouds ...

Harris wrote reams and reams of such poetry, impressive
enough for a local miner. He was also capable of moving and
emotional pieces like his poem *'On the Death of My Daughter
Lucretia (aged six years and five months)'*

And art thou gone so soon?
And is thy loving, gentle spirit fled?
Ah! is my fair, my passing beautiful,
My loved Lucretia number'd with the dead?
Ah! art thou gone so soon?

Then, of course, there are more sophisticated figures, such as
"Q', the familiar *nom de plume* for Sir Arthur Quiller Couch,
author of all those best-selling Victorian novels of life in a
Cornish fishing port. Fowey was the original for Troy Town,
and 'Q' lived there most of his life, being Mayor on more than
one occasion. He would often have well-known authors down
to stay with him, one of the most notable being Kenneth
Grahame, later to win fame for his book *The Wind in the
Willows*. Since neither 'Q' nor Kenneth Grahame were ever
associated particularly with Land's End at least in their work
(many times, of course, they paid visits for pleasure)
regretfully I cannot pursue their careers here. It was however
about this period that 'Q' founded and edited the *Cornish
Magazine*, an example which some sixty years later I
endeavoured to emulate with the *Cornish Review*. Both
magazines now lie dead and buried on public library shelves,
but it may be fitting to conclude this particular chapter with a
brief introduction to one of 'Q''s most valued contributors,
who used Newlyn as the setting for many of his stories.

Charles Lee, for that was his name, is by no means the elemental and mysterious writer such as many of those considered so far – nevertheless he is in many ways archetypical of a whole breed of authors of that period who might be said to have replaced the mystery with humour, the elemental with the human. (H.D. Lowry is another good example.) It has been said that the Cornish people combine strength and ruggedness of character with an innate shrewdness and cunning, naivity with subtlety, fire and ice in the same temperament, taciturnity with a love of rhetoric, candour with caution, open-heartedness with an ability to shut up oyster-like in an instant if the visitor seems about to take a liberty. For any writer to capture the essence of such a people would surely seem at least as difficult as to capture the essence of the Cornish landscape itself – yet this is what, almost miraculously, Charles Lee managed to do in a series of novels and short stories which he produced in a startling though brief outflow.

This is how it happened. Early in this century Charles Lee was drawn down to West Cornwall, living in the Lamorna Valley and then in Newlyn, and became so struck by the life he found down there that he made up his mind to make use of this material literally all around him. Rather after the fashion of the great Arnold Bennett, he bought a wad of notebooks and started taking down notes of what he heard and saw in the cottages where he stayed. It was as 'a chiel amang ye taking notes' that as a mixture of reporter, anthropologist and literary artist he recorded the Cornish people's habits, their nuances and their tricks of speech, so giving his tales their unique and authentic flavour. That he succeeded is testified to by no less an authority than 'Q' himself who wrote in a preface, about *The Widow Woman*, how he opened the book at home 'and hailed at once a writer who could use our speech as we natives use it, understand our ways generally, who – perhaps above all – justified himself as an artist'.

The Widow Woman, one of Charles Lee's best novels, presented a truthful portrait of what life was like in a fishing port on the Land's End peninsula at the turn of the century.

He showed the set pattern for behaviour in this place (Newlyn, in fact, called Pendennack in the book) and how it was because the conduct of the comfortably-bodied and moneyed Mrs Pollard went against the accepted local code that she failed in her ambitions. How could she expect that the young widower would prefer her, wealth and all, to the servant maid? No wonder Billy Jenkin, whom Mrs Pollard rejects in favour of John, complains, 'Mis' Pollard, your conduck edn' but light'. Her conduct in fact, would have undermined the social values and altered the sexual standards of life at Pendennack.

There was a pattern to life, still conditioned by Methodism. There was a *proper* way of courting, whether young or middle aged. The married man shaved on Sunday morning before church. The man who was looking for a wife, on the other hand, shaved on Saturday night – it being important he should present a clean smooth face to the girl of his choice! The ritual was almost tribal and woe betide anyone who tried to flout the conventions.

Apparently some critics of the time blamed Charles Lee for using too facetious a form of humour to hold up the action – but this was blaming a writer for being in harmony with his age (the late Victorian times when an Englishman still had his dignity). Charles Lee's style is really quite appropriate, as it is again in *Our Little Town*, another marvellous comic novel of life among the fishermen and their wives. There is in this book a 'battle of the Amazons', when the women attack their menfolk in that citadel of masculinity, the local cobbler's shop. Possibly Mr Lee does show signs of some male chauvinism, in that his women always seem curiously inferior to the men, but at least he has a comical way of sugaring the pill – as in this quotation from one of numerous richly Cornish characters, Uncle Hannibal in *The Widow Woman*:

When a chap an' a maid to come together, chap shuts his eyes tight; maid aupens hers a bit wider. How should a chap look to have a chanst? Man's human, but woman's woman – 'at's what I'd say in my smart way.

Reading Charles Lee's stories one is constantly coming across echoes of old rituals – like, in 'Dorinda's Birthday', the local custom in many Cornish villages such as Mousehole or Newlyn of allowing young people a few hours 'liberty' once a year on the local feast day (comparable one supposes with similar customs in Wales and Scotland). In some places couples were permitted to go off on what became known as the 'serpentine walk'. Either way it provided good material for comical events: on her seventeenth birthday Dorinda has an incredible series of amorous adventures – but decides in the end to stick to her intended.

Above all, Lee is successful in a form of irony well suited to the Cornish scene. There is always a distrust of letting the heart rule the head, as in the short story 'Mr Sampson' where a man takes a cottage next door to two spinster sisters who start quarrelling over him. Mr Sampson, however, will have none of it; he doesn't really trust his heart – 'mazy old organ, b'lieve'.

The interesting point about Charles Lee is that he came to Cornwall when he was quite young, gathered all his material during the few years he lived there – during which time, incidentally, he mixed socially a great deal with the Newlyn artists – and then went away back to settle in Hertfordshire. He wrote his handful of what many would regard as Cornish classics – and there it ended. For the rest of his life, a matter of *half a century*, not another word did he write about Cornwall. Yet, obviously, tracing these earlier and younger days, here was a classic case of Cornwall doing something that it has done for many another sensitive writer and artist – it liberated the spirit. Somehow it unlocked a door upon a creative outburst which gave us *The Widow Woman, Our Town, Paul Carah, Dorinda's Birthday, The Strong Man* and many other stories.

The fact that these stories were down to earth, slightly bawdy comical everyday stories (in some ways reminiscent of a writer such as W.W. Jacobs), does not detract from their right to consideration in this survey. Quite the contrary. Just as some painters depict Cornwall as a photograph, whereas others see abstractism as the only way of capturing the moods – so among writers there have been infinite variations on a theme, as it were. From Tennyson to Charles Lee may seem a long way, but not really. Both reacted according to their integral abilities to an outside stimulus too powerful to ignore. The world of Land's End ...

III

The Artists Come to Cornwall

During the eighteenth and nineteenth centuries, as we have
seen, the bulk of literary activity at Land's End seems to have
been connected either with the end of the land itself, or centres
such as Penzance. At the turn of the century an event took
place which was to shift some of the literary interest to the
rather different world of the fishing ports of Newlyn and
Mousehole and nearby lovely Lamorna Cove. This event was
the descent upon West Cornwall of 'them artists' – in short the
setting up of the Newlyn School of Artists, including among
them several experts of the written word as well as the
painter's brush.

What happened was that a group of ambitious young
painters who had been working over in Brittany under the
influence of Jean-François Millet and Bastien Lepage decided
to attempt to set up a similar centre in England. Cornwall has
many historical and geographical similarities with Brittany,
as well as the same warm climate, and it is easy to imagine
how the young hopefuls – among them Walter Langley, T.C.
Gotch, Frank Bramley, Percy Craft, Chevalier Taylor and the
founder, Stanhope Forbes and his wife Elizabeth – travelled
eagerly down to this new world of a picturesque fishing village
unspoiled by industrialism where they could find not only
cheap living but plenty of colourful models among the fishing
folk as well as all the vivid background they could wish for.

In an article published in the *Cornish Magazine* in 1898
Stanhope Forbes has left us this picture of those early days:

These were the days of unflinching realism, of the cult of

Bastien Lepage. It was part of our artistic creed to paint our pictures directly from Nature and not merely to rely upon sketches and studies which we could afterwards amplify in the comfort of a studio. This imparted a noticeable feature to local life. Artists are common enough objects by the seaside; but it was scarcely so usual to see the painter not merely engaged upon a small sketch or panel, but with a large canvas securely fastened to some convenient boulder, absorbed in the very work with which he hoped to win fame in the ensuing spring; perhaps even the model posing in full view of the entire populace, the portrait being executed with a publicity calculated to unnerve even our practised brother of the pavement.

These singular goings-on of the newcomers at first provoked much comment from the inhabitants but by degrees they grew familiar with such strange doings, and scarce heeded the work which progressed before their eyes. Nothing, indeed, could exceed the good nature with which the local folk came to regard behaviour which might well have been thought intrusive on the part of any others than the members of our craft. Painters have an easy way of walking into other people's houses, calmly causing their occupants no little inconvenience yet I scarcely ever remember asking permission to set up my easel without it being freely accorded.

'Do 'ee want me to set for 'ee?' soon became a common remark among the Newlyn fishermen and their wives and daughters, many of whom became quite well known as models in such large-scale canvases as Forbes' 'A Fish Sale on a Cornish Beach', Walter Langley's 'Never morning were to evening but some heart did break', T.C. Gotch's 'Sharing Fish', Frank Bramley's 'For Such is the Kingdom of Heaven' and Chevalier Taylor's 'Girl shelling peas in a Garden'. Often, it must be remembered, both models and painters worked under most difficult conditions – Stanhope Forbes shuddered at his recollection of what he endured fighting with the east wind before a large canvas on the cold and sloppy beach between Newlyn and Penzance as he worked on his fish sale painting, and Norman Garstin, after spending many long and wearisome hours on his famous view of Penzance Promenade, 'The Rain it Raineth Every Day', commented wryly, 'Your work cannot really be good unless you have caught a cold doing it'.

Among the many artists who settled around Newlyn, Mousehole and the surrounding areas there was soon quite a colony living in one of Cornwall's most noted beauty spots, Lamorna Cove. This is a lovely valley which wanders between trees down to a typically quaint, little Cornish quayside; on the way down there is a series of picturesque cottages, many of which were taken over or built originally by artists (some of them still so occupied). Lamorna Birch, a painter who actually added the village name to his own, was one of the best known painters associated with the area. Others were Ernest and Dod Procter and Harold Knight and his wife Laura, later Dame Laura Knight.

Laura Knight was not merely an outstanding painter of her day, but a writer too and her autobiography, *The Magic of a Line*, includes some delightful portraits of life in a Cornish art colony at the turn of the century. It is also fascinating for its expression of the impact of West Cornwall upon a painter's eye. Great was the joy of attempting to paint the impossible, she says, reflecting on the almost incomparable beauty of Mount's Bay. This of course was the time of outdoor painting and so she remembers always wearing a good weatherproof coat and a pair of stout hobnailed boots. Then what excitements awaited!

Today by force of elemental passion nature has opened her own paint box. See her sweep across the landscape a blue black of storm! Now watch her efface that darkness with a brushful of gold. Of colour multifarious is this frame to Mount's Bay whose turbulent waters mirror the sky. 'Guy down your canvas with more stone-filled paint rags,' I urged myself. 'Let your own brush ride in harmony with the mood of the wild.' I discovered the ecstasy of slinging paint without other thought or motive coming between. I am sure this extraordinary moment comes in the life of every artist: let the pencil or brush speak of its own accord to tell the little one can ever know.

Laura Knight declared that she doubted if anybody or anything could ever lessen the magic possessed by that far leg of land which, kicking free of the ordinary with its granite boot, defied the Atlantic Ocean. Neither time nor the vulgar would conquer its indubitable spirit. When she looked at the gorse bush on a stone hedge it seemed to her that the armoured branches forced their golden spires to the very skies as an offering of passion, of spring, to the virgin blue.

Cornwall is not like any other sort of country – it's no use trying to compare it with any other place. There are times when you think everything is quite ordinary; and there are times when you feel you are not properly you, but someone else whom you don't in the least know; and an atmosphere prevails which takes away any sense or belief you have ever had, and you don't know why, but you aren't in England any more. Once you start thinking about that undeniable mystery around you it would be better to stop or before you know where you are, it will take control and you may do something absolutely silly ... almost bound to arouse that sneaky cheeky ghost who will come and pull the plait of your hair in the night or make my dog Tip growl like hell; and down some dark lane at night you know perfectly well or you think you do, that there are no solid living objects except Tip and you, and then one of those tickly spider web things spans your face – the ones that stretch from hedge to hedge – you're absolutely certain that it's only that ghost fellow being saucy again, because you stopped to try to find one of those fire-fly bugs he holes up in the hawthorn hedge to give light enough for him to see to do his dirty mischief, half frightening Tip and you to death in that absurd manner that went out of date hundreds of years ago, and you know perfectly well that it isn't true anyway.

In those early Cornish years Laura Knight gained a reputation as a painter of nudes, many being exhibited at the Royal Academy; the most famous and the largest was 'Daughter of the Sun', priced £600, a formidable price in those pre-First World War days. Her book contains some delightful memories of hiring beautiful models and cycling out to the rocks at Lamorna, there to pose them nude in the golden sunlight. One girl in particular proved an inspiration, a Tanagra Greek statuette come to life. When the girl stopped to smell honeysuckle Laura idly said;

'It has a lovely perfume, doesn't it?'

'Yes,' replied the girl in a matter-of-fact manner, 'It smells exactly like Mr Jones's shaving soap.'

From Laura Knight's book, it is evident that the Newlyn artists led a lively social life and there are many other contemporary accounts of wild goings on: Stanhope Forbes remembered a feast in his studio from which at two in the morning, led by Walter Langley playing his banjo, a group of painters including Bramley, Hall, Craft, Todd, Millard and Fortescue marched through the village singing heartily 'As we went home by the light of the moon'. Despite such joviality the local inhabitants seem to have soon acquired a tolerance towards and indeed a respect for their new neighbours – so much so that more than a thousand Newlyn folk would flock to the annual March 'Open Days' on Newlyn meadow, looking through the studios, chatting on the grass, drinking tea and eating cakes provided for them in the open air.

There had to be limits, of course. When on one occasion at St Ives Louis Grier appeared on the wharf and set up his easel and prepared to paint a picture *on a Sunday*, it was soon made clear to him in no uncertain terms by the local fishing folk that if he dared to do this again he and his easel would find themselves in the harbour!

Such pleasant days occur less often in Newlyn and St Ives since art has now become more of a big business and somehow one doubts if that same initial flavour of innocence can be remembered. In those far off days, of course, country life was far more 'back to nature' – one of the features Laura Knight remembered was the prevalence of a bevy of local tramps who, smart fellows that they were, soon earned themselves useful money posing as models. The most famous of these tramps was actually also a professional author, W.H. Davies, author of *The Autobiography of a Super Tramp*.

To judge by Davies' charm and conversational powers alone one might say he would be at home in any sphere; but behind that seeming ease was the heart of a tramp. We never knew which of his talents gave him more pride. The glamour of having been called the author of 'some of the finest lyrics in the English language' could never entirely efface the vagrant who had been driven from back door to imprisonment.

In the summer of 1922 Davies went down to Cornwall and stayed with Harold and Laura Knight in one of their Lamorna studios. Apparently for a long time he was content just to sit for hours in the sunshine, doing nothing. Later on, however, he became annoyed at the sight of the wilderness of stunted bushes and small trees around the studios. 'Such timber going to waste – what me, a tramp, not to put it to use!' In no time he had all his friends hard at work and was teaching them the arts of lighting big bonfires.

Every evening our bonfire was attended by artists and their families. Davies arranged it to smoke, flare and blaze up to an exact timetable. Each night at twelve o'clock, when it reached the glowing ember stage, to his disappointment we would all go to our beds. He wanted us to stay there all night with our feet turned to the heat, but he, the erstwhile tramp, dreading to do the wrong thing, would also go back to sleep in his shed ... Our indulgence was a frequent pot of tea and gingerbread biscuits, while Davies, aglow in flame and pride, trimmed the bonfire with a branch. One evening Robert Newton, then aged fourteen, gave a vicious kick to the bonfire, spoiling its perfection; Davies, the conductor, put down his baton in a fit of sulks. 'That lad will live to be a sorrow to his mother! Don't you think I am ever going to forgive that Bobby Newton for the mischief he has done.'

At the end of the war Harold Knight decided it was time to pull out of Cornwall and return to London. His wife had a passionate love of the sea and was appalled at the thought of having nothing to do but look at bricks, concrete and chimney pots – however, in retrospect she commented that Harold had been right, and that Cornwall in beauty so fancified was an easy part of the country for an artist to sleep in.

Nevertheless it hardly seems that there was much time for sleeping during the sojourn at Newlyn of so many busy artists at work – a fact commented on by another literary figure of those days, Bernard Walke, the vicar of St Hilary and author of that engaging autobiography *Twenty Years At St Hilary*. During his incumbency Walke set out to beautify his church by commissioning paintings from Ernest Procter, Dod Procter, Harold Harvey, Harold Knight, Norman Garstin and many others of the Newlyn group. Ernest Procter did a striking altar piece in the Chapel of Our Lady and a picture of the deposition from the Cross above the altar of the Holy Souls. Perhaps the most remarkable works were provided by a young girl, Joan Manning Sanders who at the age of nine was already proposing to illustrate the whole of the Old Testament. Bernard Walke regarded her paintings as the quintessence of childhood and they were put on the parclose screen of the Lady Chapel and can be seen to this day.

Twenty Years at St Hilary is too diffuse a book to be paraphrased here, but it provides a fascinating reconstruction of quite a wide stratum of Cornish social life, for as a parish priest Bernard Walke had contacts with all classes and had an especial rapport with the ordinary Cornish miners and workers. His wife, Annie, was a painter and he himself had many contacts in the literary world, so that the rambling old vicarage at St Hilary was often host to such figures as Compton Mackenzie, Filson Young, E.F. Benson, Walter de La Mare, Roger Fry, Harold and Laura Knight, the Manning-Sanders, A.J. Munnings, Dod and Ernest Procter,

Stanhope Forbes, and Percy Lubbock, to name but a few.
There was even a surprise visit from Bernard Shaw who called
in to see the annual Christmas Play at the church and stayed
after for a cup of tea. Walke introduced him to the painter
Norman Garstin, another Irishman.

Norman Garstin opened the conversation in his most
courteous manner, saying that he and Shaw had several
things in common. 'And what might they be? asked Shaw
quizzically. 'Why, I am an Irishman, Mr Shaw – and I, too,
am an admirer of Bernard Shaw.'

Bernard Walke was a close friend of Compton Mackenzie and
he and Annie often visited the novelist and his wife Faith when
they lived at 'a great gloomy house surrounded by tall elms at
Phillack, near Hayle'.

On windy days in the autumn we flew kites on the sand
dunes overlooking St Ives and after dinner, if we were
staying the night, as often we did, we would all go to a
room, high up and overlooking Hayle Estuary, called The
Lady's Bower, where Faith would play the piano while
Monty wrote *Carnival* and I lay on the floor and built
cathedrals and castles from an inexhaustible supply of toy
building bricks that Mackenzie had obtained from
Germany and of which he was very proud. I would sit on
and build while Mackenzie wrote, long after Annie and
Faith had gone to bed, sometimes until two in the morning,
when Mackenzie would read me the chapter he had
written ...
   Once Annie and I were invited to a dinner given by Faith
and Monty to celebrate the publication of *Carnival*. We rode
over on bicycles early in the afternoon and after tea
Mackenzie and I visited the cellars (reported to have a
secret passage to the sea) and selected several bottles of
champagne and two bottles of the port his father had laid
down some years previously. We did not wait for dinner to
drink to Jenny Pearl, but opened a bottle of champagne in

the hall and Martin Secker, the publisher, proposed a toast of success to *Carnival*.

Another personality who seems to have impressed Bernard Walke was at that time living and painting over at Lamorna Cove, Sir Alfred Munnings.

Leaning up against the bay horse was a man in a flannel shirt without a collar wiping paint brushes with a rag: it was this man who attracted my attention. The poise of his body and the tilt of his head as he leaned against the horse watching our arrival suggested an arrogant, almost insolent attitude towards the strangers who were approaching. Here, I thought, was a man whom I should most certainly dislike, when Ernest Procter, seeing us eyeing one another, introduced me and said 'This is A.J. Munnings'.

The man in the flannel shirt looked even more insolent and then as if he had relented, threw back his head and smiled a queer smile giving the impression that his face had been lit up from within. The term smile does not adequately convey my meaning, for there is something of a conscious effort in a smile. What I saw then, and have seen many times since, was the invasion of a face by a vivid personality. At other times his is the face of a man who has spent his life with horses, but, lit with that smile, it is the face of an aesthetic saint … He approaches literature with the freshness with which he looks at a landscape and will describe what he has read with the same vividness as a scene he has witnessed. Never before have I met a man who gave so liberally of his personality. Wherever he lives or whatever company he keeps he remains at heart a countryman. He has never forsaken the land: he looks at it and loves it, its pasture and plough, its cattle and horses, its villages and old churches, as a countryman loves these things.

Towards the latter part of his time at St Hilary, Bernard Walke became nationally known through the BBC broadcasts of the Christmas Play, an event which came about through his friendship with the broadcaster Filson Young, who used to stay over at Carbis Bay. On the first occasion with the church piled high with batteries, a switchboard, a telephone and BBC engineers everywhere, Bernard Walke remembers feeling anxious until the moment came for his bellringers to break into action.

> From that moment I had no feeling of anxiety only a sense of exultation as I heard the bells ring out above the roaring of the gale. Never at any other time have I been so conscious of the wonder of the world. Over the High Altar burned a white light proclaiming the presence of the Incarnate God whose nativity we were celebrating while above our heads was another light burning red, warning the players that any sounds within the church were at that moment being transmitted over the face of the earth. The strangeness of the church with the batteries, engineers from London and overhead wires had gone. There remained the angel who was standing beneath the arch of the tower looking very lovely with gold and silver wings and uplifted hand waiting to proclaim the news of man's salvation, and Peter on his knees in the straw, with my cloak now fallen from his shoulders and his old hands uplifted in supplication. Time had fled and left me with the angel Gabriel and an old shepherd somewhere on the plains near Bethlehem.

Bernard Walke goes on to describe how at the end of those broadcasts everyone gathered in the big old kitchen at the vicarage for a great evening of conviviality. By a strange coincidence some decades later I and my family went to live at that same Old Vicarage, St Hilary, and spent five very happy years there, and this is what we, too, have uppermost in our minds – memories of great gatherings, either in the old farmhouse style kitchen or in the big almost baronial sitting room where every evening there was always a huge log fire burning. It would seem almost as if, no doubt influenced by the character and experiences of Bernard Walke and his circle, that strange old building was deduced to be a social refuge, a centre for gaiety and happiness – a place where artists and writers of the district could come and replenish their social batteries, so to speak, before returning once more to explore the mysteries of the countryside around them.

Compton Mackenzie and his wife Faith had first arrived in Cornwall towards the end of 1907, staying then with the renowned and eccentric 'Perpetual Curate of Cury-in-Gunwalloe', the Reverend Sandys Wason, at a rent of £1 a week each 'excluding wine and washing'. Although fascinated by that remarkable church at Gunwalloe which is literally washed by great Atlantic waves at high tide, and intrigued by all the local tales of treasure trove to be found in the district, Mackenzie does not appear to have been really settled at Cury.

However, it was here that an important event took place in his life as a writer. Previously a poet and a playwright and uncertain quite of what to do next, he was walking home to the vicarage when suddenly he made up his mind he would write a novel! As he recounts in an early volume of *My Life and Times*, he then hurried back to the vicarage and there by the light of two candles began a novelisation of a play he had once written, *The Gentleman in Grey* – later to appear as his novel *The Passionate Elopement*.

While still living at Gunwalloe, Compton Mackenzie was asked by his mother to find her a suitable Cornish home – which he did, at Riviere House, Phillack, a large imposing house built by one of the Hayle 'copper-barons' (it actually had a copper roof). For a while the Mackenzies paid regular visits to Riviere House – 'on our weekly drive of fifteen miles from Gunwalloe in a dog-cart we seldom met more than one car, when our little groom would jump down to hold the mare's head until the fearful vehicle had passed'* but in the end it seemed more convenient for them all to move in together. There then began a most productive period for the author, both creatively and socially. On the latter front there

* *My Life and Times*, Chatto & Windus.

were visits from Bernard and Annie Walke of St Hilary, from Hugh Walpole over at Truro (used as setting for the *Herries Chronicles*) and from Charles Marriott, art critic of *The Times* and author of *The Column*. In his *Memories of the Art Colonies* Marriott recalls frequently entertaining the Mackenzies and how his friend and fellow author Hugh Walpole took part in cricket matches with the artists.

On the creative front, having finished his first novel Compton Mackenzie conceived a second one – as it was to be, his first best-seller, *Carnival*. In his memories he recollects tha: the inspiration for this novel came from a meeting with a Cornish farmer, 'a tall gaunt dark man' who had married a London barmaid. He decided to build up a story of a girl, Jenny Pearl, who would marry Zachary Trewhella, a Cornish farmer, and that the farmer would kill her in the last chapter. The novel, an immediate success, was actually printed at Plymouth and the publisher Martin Secker came with Mackenzie to preside at the stopping of the presses after the first thousand copies had been produced so that the next thousand could legitimately be called a 'second impression'.

Although his life in West Cornwall was confined to about seven years Compton Mackenzie took quite an active part in local affairs. He was in fact tempted to enter the priesthood and got so far as being licensed as a lay reader, after ordination at Truro Cathedral. He also diligently travelled around the county exploring various places of interest though few fascinated him more than that on his own doorstep, the weird and haunting sands of Gwithian.

Once while on his travels he stayed at Fowey where he acted in a local production of *The Merchant of Venice* directed by the great 'Q', Sir Arthur Quiller Couch, a writer Mackenzie admired greatly. Gardening was another intense interest: he even thought of setting up as a professional gardener at Riviere House, which had a large area of land around it suitable for cultivation. During his time there he actually planted more than 3,000 differen: varieties of shrubs, plants and bulbs, among them the best white trumpet daffodil of the day, priced at £30 a bulb.

In due course Compton Mackenzie followed up *Carnival* with another success, *Sinister Street*, also written at Riviere House. Then in 1913 he and his wife decided to leave Cornwall and live abroad on Capri, the first of many island homes. However he has left many fascinating records of his Cornish observations from which it is clear that many of the ideas later worked into novels – perhaps, for instance, *Whisky Galore* may well have had originations in explorations along the wild Cornish coasts. For instance, the author recalls having heard rumours of a ship having been wrecked at Helzephron Cove and that a number of soldiers were thought to have been drowned through having filled their helmets with gold they were reluctant to part with. These men had been buried according to the custom then prevailing on the cliff top above the cove and Compton Mackenzie describes how he was approached by a couple of local lads to help in recovering the gold. On a dark night they duly met, but at the last moment his two companions were suddenly overcome with fear at the thoughts of all kinds of ghostly visitations and threw down their long-handled spades and fled to the safety of their homes.

On another occasion, also at Helzephron, Mackenzie was fortunate enough to be present on the last day of the annual Huers' watch for mullet. Suddenly the cry went up, 'Heva! Heva! Heva!' He ran with the rest of the local fishermen to help launch the boats and was given a seat in the cock boat whose job it was to direct the casting of the seine net. The catch that day was a formidable one, valued at more than £200, and Mackenzie made sure to note down the details of his unusual experience for later use in one of his books. He seems, in short, to have been one of those professional writers who, though their period in West Cornwall was relatively short, responded avidly to the impact of all the wild and majestic imagery around him.

At the time the Newlyn artists were establishing themselves around the western end of Mount's Bay one of their number, Norman Garstin, was discovering that his son showed talents for a different art form. Crosbie Garstin was born in 1887 at

Penzance and in his earlier life was something of a wanderer, working in Canada as a bronco-buster, later in Bechuanaland and finally returning to Europe to enlist in the army for the First World War. During this period he wrote poetry and his poems appeared in *Punch*, the *Spectator, Pall Mall Gazette*, and later in book form as *Vagabond Verses*. After the war he went off on another foreign adventure a tour of Spain and Morocco, and it was the notes he kept on this trip that gave him the idea, back in Cornwall, of trying his hand at a novel, *The Coasts of Romance*.

After this appeared there was no stopping him: as he said himself, he was intensely interested in people, loved travel, and had hundreds of plots buzzing around in his head. What's more he had a powerful narrative style that carried the reader along impressively – a factor testified to by the incident of his publisher, on receiving what was intended to be the final chapter of a Cornish novel, *The Owl's House*, telegramming 'Re-write last chapter. Penhale too good a character to kill off!'

The Owl's House, together with *High Noon* and *The West Wind*, which make up Garstin's Cornish *Penhale* trilogy, are the books on which his reputation stands. In many ways they are predecessors to Winston Graham's *Poldark* books: although Garstin's deal with farming and Graham's with mining there are many similarities between the main protagonists, John Penhale and Ross Poldark, both dark brooding figures with scars and wilful ways and terrible tempers. Like Graham, Garstin held authenticity of detail in great importance and believed in saturating himself in the technical background. He could write most vividly, as is demonstrated on almost every page of *The Owl's House*. For instance, in this account of John Penhale riding through the night and remembering a previous occasion when the Squire's daughter ran away from him, sobbing, panting, stumbling in furrows, torn by brambles:

The moon was flying through clouds like a circus-girl through hoops: the road was swept by winged shadows.

Puddles seemed to brim with milk at one moment, ink the next. At one moment the surrounding country was visible, a-gleam as with hoar frost, and then was blotted out in darkness: it was a night of complete and startling transformations. The shadow of a bare oak leapt upon them suddenly, flinging unsubstantial arms at man and horse as though to grasp them, a phantom octopus. Penhale's mare shied, nearly unseating him. He came out of his sombre thoughts, kicked spurs into her and drove her on at a smart trot. She swung forward trembling and uneasy, nostrils swelling, ears twitching, as though she sensed uncanny presences abroad.

Although he travelled extensively, and brought his travels into many of his novels, such as *The Dragon and the Lotus*, Cornwall was always Crosbie Garstin's first love. And in more ways than one for, romantically, he met his wife, Lillian, through an incident at Lamorna Cove when Lillian's sister Althea got into difficulties swimming and was rescued by the author – as a reward the sister flung her arms around him and within a few weeks they were engaged. Appropriately enough, Lamorna was the place the Garstins chose to live in at first, occupying the first of the small row of cottages that face the sea on the little jetty down by the harbour. Later they moved further up the valley in a house not far from the Merry Maidens, near St Buryan.

For four years the Garstins lived happily and Crosbie prospered as a writer; then his career, already so successful, came to a tragic end. He had been working under great pressure to finish *The West Wind*, the last of the *Penhale* trilogy, and finally completed the manuscript and sent the manuscript off to his publishers. At that moment the Holman family invited Garstin to join them on a trip in their yacht up the Cornish and Devon coast, an offer that must have seemed a blessed relief after all that concentrated work. At Salcombe when the others went ashore he stayed aboard; however later on he too rowed to the town.

It was returning in a small 'pram' boat together with two

companions that the tragedy happened: the 'pram' began to sink, one member of the party swum to shore for help while the other, a young lady, later said she owed her life to the fact that 'invisible hands' removed her coat and helped her to get back to land. Alas, in the process of saving the young lady's life Crosbie Garstin lost his own – presumed drowned though, to add to the mystery, his body was never found.

It is a strange irony that in the closing pages of *The West Wind* Ortho Penhale prefers death to capture:

> The boom of the surf was the deep roll of drums. The wind blew with the sound of trumpets, piercing, exultant. The phantom clippers dipped their gilded beaks, most stately, the ghostly soldiers tossed their lances, 'Come on, old comrade,' they cried. 'Fear not! Death is but a pang and life immortal. Ride on with us, ride on for ever!' A roller surged over the rock ledges, up and up, wrapping white foam about Ortho's knees; spume flakes spattered his bare chest, flecked his black bull curls. He flung both hands towards the rising sun in salute – and plunged.

Newlyn and Lamorna by no means held a monopoly of literary activities in the early part of the century. Many writers were, as ever, still drawn further down the south-western end of the coast.

> On the western tip of Cornwall the broad sands of Whitesand Beach stretch in an unbroken band from Aire Point to Sennen Cove at low tide. As the sea rises each bay becomes cut off and enclosed by its own cliffs, and waves roll in from the Atlantic sometimes as high as a house, breaking on the huge rounded boulders piled like giant marbles behind the sands. When there is frost in the air and a biting wind coming in off the sea you will find yourself alone if you make the rough descent to the beach. Whitesand Bay shows the power and splendour of the sea, the scale of rocks, sky and ocean and the fragility of man. The lifeboatmen at Sennen have performed some of the

most skilful and heroic rescues ever recorded. If you stand on the rocks and look across the sea you can feel, even on a fine day, something of what they are up against. In spring the small fields terraced down the western slope of the cliff come alive with daffodils and the Isles of Scilly are distinctly seen on a clear day. This is the time to find the lonely places on the coast to walk for miles along the sands without meeting or passing anyone.

This extract from *Coastline*, an artist's impression of a journey round England and Wales by Kenneth Lindley, aptly sums up one of the most renowned areas of Penwith, Land's End itself. It would be surprising if such an area had not appealed to the imaginations of a wide range of visiting writers and artists. Apart from the poems and letters and essays which such visits produced there emerged, then and during the turn of the century, a whole spate of romantic novels which made full use of the splendour and fearfulness of the setting. Among these was *In the Roaring of the Sea* by S. Baring Gould, *Amorel, A Story of Lyonesse* by Walter Besant and numerous novels by Silas and Joseph Hocking.

Perhaps one of the most famous of all these novels is still a best-seller to this day, cheerfully earning reprint after reprint nearly 100 years after it was written. This is *The Watchers of the Longships* by J.F. Cobb, a story into which almost all the ingredients of a popular soap opera have been liberally poured: lonely lighthouse keeper, the girl who loves him, the minister torn by religious doubts, villains of various sorts – plus, and this is the important point and probably explains the novel's continued sales, a truly melodramatic reconstruction of what it really is like to live at a hard, lonely, sea-threatened finger of land poking out into the face of the huge Atlantic swell, like Sennen Cove.

Arthur Symons, author of *Spiritual Adventures* and *Cities and Sea, Coasts and Islands*, a friend of Aubrey Beardsley, Oscar Wilde and others flourishing in English literary life around the turn of the century, was another well-known writer who felt constantly drawn to the Land's End area. He loved West

Cornwall in all weathers, rain, mist and the sunshine after rain, and once recorded the delights of going down on the beach after a day of rain and seeing a line of white foam around the whole coast edging a sea which has turned to a strange leaden green, veiled with sea mist. Land's End itself continually fascinated:

> In this remote, rocky and barren land there is an essential solitude which nothing, not the hotel, nor the coming and going of people in the middle of the day, can disturb. Whenever I get right out to the last point of the rocks, where one looks straight down as if between walls of granite, to the always white and chafing water, I feel at once alone and secure, like a bird in the cleft of the rock. There is the restfulness of space, the noise of sea birds and the sea, and nothing else but silence. In this solitude, away from the people of cities, one learns to be no longer alone.

Symons was representative of a number of writers who visited Cornwall at regular intervals. On the other hand, as is not really surprising, there have been many other writers who, to misquote a famous saying, 'came, saw – and stayed'. Many of these settled around Whitesand Bay, in the little village of Sennen Cove. It was here during the last few years of her life in the early part of this century that a now forgotten woman novelist of impressive talent (placed by eminent critics of her time alongside D.H. Lawrence and T.S. Eliot) lived in a little bungalow. Mary Butts was at one time part of the same general world of bohemia as other women writers like Virginia Woolf and Dorothy Richardson: indeed earlier in her life she lived in Paris and mixed with Jean Cocteau and other great literary figures of France. She wrote novels and short stories, and many of the latter were about Cornwall, or, as she sometimes called her settings, the Land of Bolerium, where Land's End and Pendeen boom and hoot in the writhing mists. In her story 'Look Homeward, Angel' there is this vivid passage:

The lovers sat, side by side, building up their fire; and Julian laid across it a bleached log of driftwood, to burn with a white flame and spitting blue sparks, charring to a silk ash over a core of rose. Contented they sat together in the old house in the secret valley above the sea. Outside the stream ran, singing its full-throated mid-winter song; outside the night was blind with sea fog, windless mist, made visible by the light streaming from the windows as if made of myriad diamond points. Since dusk it had entered their valley, rising off the sea, brimming the tiny cove, rising past the mill to their house enclosed in its trees and its garden where the flowers bloomed the whole year long. Past them, it had risen across the moors, to the dreadful hills with their standing stones. Avenues and circles and huts and stones of sacrifice – of a race which has by no means died out in the 'Extreme West'.

Here is a writer strongly influenced by her physical surroundings: indeed she goes on to describe how the stillness might be broken by man's answer to the day and night terrors of fog at sea when the sirens at Pendeen Lighthouse answered the gun on the Longships, muffled thunder alternating with a strangled moan for even these huge voices 'the fog had by the throat and men heard them as one might imagine voices from the other side of death'. Almost every line of the story is permeated strongly with the local atmosphere, such as a reference to Wolf Rock as the last stone in England standing up out of the sea like a black tooth. When her husband speaks, he wonders why millions of drops of water are a reason why large iron ships should pile up on rocks and be ground to pieces on equally hard stones. The story itself has suitably haunting undertones as it delicately tells the tale of the drowning at sea of the girl's lover and his apparent return his figure outlined 'in that light that shines or grows in dyke or ditch nor yet in any sheugh – but at the gates of Paradise'.

Paradise is hardly a word one would apply to Sennen Cove, for it is a place subject to constant buffeting by wild winds so that the local people have always lived dourly in close-knit, grey granite cottages with tiny windows. The writers who have visited or settled there, on the other hand, not having grown up in such a constantly harsh atmosphere, have tended to choose more exposed spots. Like their friend Mary Butts, the Manning Sanders, George and Ruth, lived in a pleasant large bungalow along Maria's Lane, looking out directly across Whitesand Bay to Cape Cornwall. For a time in the years between the two wars their home was quite a literary haven, and many writer friends used to stay with them, like Frank Baker, Naomi Royde Smith, Angus Davidson and Oswell Blakeston.

George Manning Sanders was both painter and writer, and a most engaging and effervescent extrovert character full of wit and liveliness – characteristics he bravely maintained even for all those years of his later life when he was confined to a motorised wheelchair (in which he would whizz rather dangerously about the narrow Land's End lanes). Himself a native of Cornwall, George Manning Sanders possessed a neat ability to capture the inner, often tortured character of the Cornish. He wrote several novels, as well as numerous articles for literary magazines, but the short story was his real love, and I published several in the *Cornish Review*. Typical of them was his 'Mother and Son', in which Mother stands at her cottage door, anxiously scanning the steep, winding hill out of the fishing cove and inevitably spies Son returning from a fishing trip with a girl as companion. When the boat grounds on the slipway the girl runs off, Son moors his boat and lumbers towards his waiting mother with a semi-guilty smile disfiguring his honest face. The tussle between the two goes on and on – when the son announces he has asked the girl to marry him, Mother replies, 'Then you might so well order me a coffin.' Inevitably the girl lets Son down and Mother happily regains control. 'Take your tea now, and scoff it down while it's hot'.

Ruth Manning Sanders, now living in retirement in Penzance in her nineties, is Welsh, not Cornish. Her writings – much more well-known and prolific than those of her late husband – have tended to focus very largely on

Cornwall, and in particular the Cornwall of myths and legends. She has written a whole series of fairy stories around these legends, illustrated by her talented painter daughter, Joan Manning Sanders. Even her more serious adult stories are strongly flavoured with the same touch of other worldliness together with a direct and vivid protrayal of the local scenery.

One stormy afternoon in late summer John took a sack and went down to the sea shore in search of wreck wood. The shore was littered with shining brown ribbons of seaweed and the wood that he gathered was all tangled up with sand and shells. Great waves staggered and broke along the shore, and the run of them swirled up around John's feet, so that sometimes he was ankle deep and sometimes high and dry. From the tops of the breakers an off-sea wind flung foam into his eyes. The low and watery sun, shooting its rays from amidst rapidly moving storm clouds, brightened the foam, and flung wide mirrors of light across the backs and amongst the hollows of the mountainous waves that rose and fell beyond the breakers. And in these waves the seals, an old one and a young one, were merrily playing. Up they floated like things of cork, and down they dived, swift as birds flying; and when they dived John saw the shadow of their bodies through the waves, and when they floated up he saw their big eyes shining.

Ruth Manning Sanders lived out on the Land's End cliffs for several decades and probably came to have a closer understanding of that area than most other writers. It becomes easier if you settle in a particular spot in Cornwall – not necessarily at Land's End (Trencrom Hill or Ding Dong or the heights above Zennor would have much the same effect) – to feel the impact upon the creative imagination made by the sheer grandeur of the setting, the whole almost indefinable atmosphere of mystery.

Sometimes on a blustery day when the wind whips at your feet and cuts into your cheeks and the sea roars and rages it would be impossible not to feel a sense of fear – especially, for instance, watching those small tankers and cargo vessels fighting their way around the turbulent waters of Land's End, marvelling that their frailty could withstand the elemental forces unleashed by rough weather. Even on such wild days the whole scene reflects a kind of terrible beauty which is paralleled only in the Western Isles of Scotland, perhaps the west coast of Ireland. Above all there lurks among all these scenes, half-hidden behind the spray and the confusion, that sense of the ultimate when, in the words of Ruth Manning Sanders, the place becomes haunted and 'a giant heaves grey limbs from his granite bed, a witch sits in that stone chair on the cliff ...'

IV

Best Sellers and Literary Giants

In any consideration of the contemporary literary scene of Land's End it is only right to give due credit to the part played by what may be called the best-seller element. After all, *Penmarric*, one of the biggest best sellers of recent years both in this country and America, was written and researched by Susan Howatch down in Cornwall, and set in typically wild and rugged Cornish countryside. There have in fact been a number of well-known names on the romantic novelists' list who have made vivid use of Cornish scenery and atmosphere: Victoria Holt, E.V. Thompson, Margaret Kennedy, Constance Heaven, etc.

However Susan Howatch is actually from Yorkshire and *Penmarric* is primarily an instance of a writer happening to use Cornwall as a backcloth for a single, rather formularised, romantic plot and (with the exception of E.V. Thompson who now lives near Bodmin) this could be said to apply to the other writers I have in mind – their connection with Cornwall is a tenuous one and so it would seem inappropriate to consider them in a particularised study of Land's End literature.

By contrast over recent years there have been a number of outstanding popular authors with world-wide reputations whose links with Cornwall are altogether stronger and more lasting, ranging from children's writers such as Angela Brazil, who lived at Polperro, and Beatrix Potter, who spent some time at Falmouth, to romantic novelists such as Howard Spring, whose best-known novels have strong Cornish settings – *My Son, My Son, Fame is the Spur, There is a House*, and notably his very last book, *Winds of the Day*. Howard Spring wrote in the main about the Falmouth area where he lived for thirty years and he had a shrewd and direct feeling for the romantic pull of Cornwall: there is a passage in *My Son, My Son,* when the hero and narrator first comes down:

> It was the first time I had travelled into the West Country and once I had crossed the Saltash Bridge leaving Devonshire behind and had entered upon the strange, riven countryside of Cornwall, with the railway passing over the viaduct carrying us above chasms filled with dusky woods, and through tilted, angular postures, and alongside the great white cones of the clay works that rose against the sky like giant's tents, and giving us here and there glimpses of the distant sea bluer than any I had known, and nearer views of unaccustomed vegetation, eucalyptus and palm and a profusion of hydrangeas; why, then I felt the North fall like a smokey burden from my back and a deep willingness for lotus eating take possession of me.

Daphne du Maurier is perhaps the most famous living example of a popular contemporary novelist whose work has served to make romantic Cornwall a household word all over the world. There can be few countries, certainly in the Western hemisphere, where there have not been published large editions of books such as *Frenchman's Creek, The King's General, Jamaica Inn, My Cousin Rachel, Rebecca, The House on the Strand,* and many of them have been made into films which have also been shown all over the world. In all these books the du Maurier touch is unmistakable: a superb storyteller she manages to reconstruct a universe in which readers can retain a measure of belief even at moments of dramatic tension, when the events and characters somehow seem to free themselves from the bond of history.

She is one of those writers who seems to soak herself into the very heart of what she is writing about – sometimes on most ambitious lines, as in *The House on the Strand,* a tale on two levels about a man living in modern Cornwall who periodically takes a drug which enables him to experience life in the Cornwall of hundreds of years back. In fact over the years Daphne du Maurier has consistently widened her frontiers as a writer, thus giving the lie to those inevitable critics who dismiss her work simply because it is popular.

What has helped Daphne du Maurier enormously in this context is the simple fact that she has lived immersed in the heart of Cornwall for nearly half a century, for most of that time at her great mansion Menabilly, near Fowey, which in many ways served as the model for the immortal 'Manderley' in *Rebecca*. She still in fact lives on the Rashleigh estate, though not at Menabilly, at the grand age of seventy-four, and it was after a visit there that her friend Noel Welch wrote a delightful portrait which I published in the *Cornish Review* and from which I quote this brief cameo:

Daphne is like the concentration of a summer day and, like Cornish summer days, which she herself has so well described, no sooner does one feel it is in one's grasp than one is left with a blue ghost (she wears blue often) blending with sea and sky, then lost in the mist, always so ready in Cornwall to snatch things away, to wrap them in its own peculiar mystery. One will probably, though, continue to hear her kindly, but mocking, laugh. She uses laughter as a builder uses the back of his hand to distinguish the true from the false, to feel out the real structure behind the brave facade Daphne is always after the real person, never mind how small and frightened and inadequate he or she may turn out to be. Ruthlessly she taps away till the genuine article is exposed. There is something of the recluse in her, something of the monk. The most surprising people come to Kilmarth but she can rarely be enticed out: her friends are hand-picked. She believes in living each phase of her life, experiencing everything, however bleak, to the full. Long ago the escape-hatches were locked, the bolt-holes stopped. She believes in the need and value of roots and regularity. She has set times for work, set times for the long walks that take her to the Gribben or Par Beach, where the beachcomber she discovered in her father combines in her with the eternal child. She is obsessed with the sea. She waits for it to come in to fill every crevice and rock pool. It is at high tide that her stories are always begun ...

Many of Daphne du Maurier's novels are set in the area of Cornwall around her home, ranging from Fowey to Bodmin in the east and to Falmouth in the west, but in fact, almost inevitably, she has been drawn as well to the mysterious end of the land. While this has not featured particularly in novels, it forms a major subject in one of the most fascinating of all her books, *Vanishing Cornwall*.

It is in this book that she underlines the fact that those who most desire to understand the Cornish and their country must use their imagination and travel back in time, for superstition flows in the blood, and rocks and stones and hills and valleys bear the imprint of men who long ago buried their dead beneath great chambered tombs ... the very stones, like the natural granite cast up from the earth by nature defy the centuries. The present vanishes, centuries dissolve, the mocking course of history with all its triumphs and defeats is blotted out. It is in this fine book Daphne du Maurier suggests:

> The right way to approach Cornwall is from the sea, sailing from southern Ireland to the Hayle estuary as the first traders did in those centuries B.C. – and surely with the same shock of surprise and relief, after a stormy passage, with the prevailing south-easterly wind veering between the quarter and hard astern, to find that the inhospitable rock-bound Cornish clay thrusting into the Atlantic in quest of victims has, to the immediate northwest of its scaly hump, a welcome haven. Then, as today, the contrast was profound between the forbidding grandeur of the coastline about Land's End, with its hinterland of granite tors, and the sudden emergence of St Ives Bay, an encircling arm protecting the shallows and the yellow sands and the estuary of Hayle; but then, unlike today, the river, broad and deep, was tidal inland for four miles or more, cutting

nearly to Mount's Bay on the south coast.

Hayle was a natural refuge, the obvious centre for a trading population who, building trackways beside the river valley, could barter their tin to vessels coming from both the Atlantic and Channel sea routes. The estuary, alas, is now, and has been through the centuries, silting up. A narrow channel, marked with straggling poles to warn the venturing seamen of the ever encroaching banks of sand, leads to the once flourishing port. Even the yachtsman dares not hazard the passage that long ago offered shelter and opportunity to Bronze Age seamen.

For the watcher today, crouching amidst the sand dunes and the tufted grass, looking seaward to where the shallows run, imagination can take a riotous course, picturing line upon line of high-prowed flat-bottomed craft, brightly coloured, their sails abeam, entering the river with the flood tide.

What cries and oaths, what turbulence of Mediterranean chatter interspersed with Irish, as the traders ran their vessels on the sand or anchored them to swing midstream; what speedy loading or unloading of cargo between ship and settlement, what feasting, when the work was done, beside a fire of turf and furze; what interchange of vows with dance and conquest. The image fades, and the dreamer, stiff from crouching in the dunes, sees how the sand has, through the centuries, invaded the coastal countryside north of Hayle. Hurricanes, in the long distant past, whipped up the swirling mass into dense clouds which settled on the land below. Whole farmsteads were overwhelmed and now lie buried, while the wasteland known as the towans – a mixture of sand and sea rush a stiff-stemmed, reedy grass planted in the old days by the inhabitants to stay the driving sand – stretches through Phillack and Gwithian parishes until the ground rises into the headland of Godrevy Point.

Gales and storms have been ever frequent on both north and south Cornish coasts, bringing havoc and disaster with them and a multitude of wrecks, but a hurricane of sand, destroying homes, was the grim fate of these Gwithian farmers near to Hayle. A winter gale will spend its force, the seas grow calm, the rains cease; the sand is a more insidious enemy. During one tempestuous winter of the nineteenth century there was a sudden shifting of the sands and the long buried farmstead of Upton was exposed to view, roof and walls preserved like a villa in Pompeii. People came from near and far to gaze in wonder. Then the wind and sand rose up in unison and Upton was buried once again.

This is fine writing by one of Cornwall's finest writers, who can also sum up her view of Cornwall in a phrase: 'Here in the lichened stone is the essence of memory itself.' No wonder that sometimes literary critics have referred to Cornwall as 'du Maurier country'!

Daphne du Maurier is not the only writer in her family. Her elder sister, Angela, who has also spent most of her life living at Fowey in a lovely black and white house which is quite a landmark on the river's edge at Bodinnick, has written a series of romantic novels and also an autobiography entitled somewhat wryly, *It's Only the Sister*; and the third sister, Jeanne, is a well-known painter, whose paintings of Cornwall adorn galleries in many countries. One way and another Cornwall has reason to be grateful to the du Mauriers.

Winston Graham is the other big Cornish best-seller of recent years, largely owing to the enormous popularity of the television adaptation of his series of *Poldark* novels, about life in a Cornish mining community of the eighteenth century. Like Daphne du Maurier, Winston Graham is not a native of Cornwall, but again like her he came to live in the county several decades ago at Perranporth on the north coast and it was there in a little writing hut out on the cliffs that he wrote many of his best-selling books which include, apart from the *Poldark* books, such international titles as *Marnie* and *Cordelia*. Much of the background of the *Poldark* stories is the wild and rugged North Cornish coast, and though originally Winston Graham had in mind some of the mines around St Agnes the similarity with the mining area of St Just is so complete that when the BBC came to make their films the film unit went down to Land's End, making use not only of Pendeen and St Just settings, but also of some of the local manor houses. One of the reasons for the enormous popularity of the *Poldark* novels is undoubtedly the meticulous research which Winston Graham put into recreating a world of long ago; the characters are all utterly convincing, and both Ross and Demelza are strongly flavoured with that aura, so difficult to define, of 'being Cornish'. There is no doubt that not only have the *Poldark* books caught the popular imagination – they have captivated Winston Graham too! He finds it impossible to give up the continuing saga and is now at work on a seventh volume, following the last, *The Angry Tide*. His writing consistently reflects his great love and understanding of Cornwall and its mysteries:

> The sandhills were a desert of salt and deep pools and ravines of shadows. Across them and through them she plunged, sometimes waist deep in darkness, sometimes in full light, her shadow like a dog at her feet. She walked as if in a dream. At the cliff she hesitated. The surf was a line of phantom cavalry, dividing sand and sea. At the bottom the sand was soft and pale and secret. The lightest of cool airs wafted and she shivered, but it was not cold. The rocks were sharp edged like witches' faces and the shadows were monstrous and misshapen. It was a midsummer's night's dream, all of it a dream, in which she walked lonely and afraid.

That extract from Winston Graham's ghost story, 'Coty's Cove', could have been written about any of the dozens of strange and secretive little coves to be found all the way round the first and last peninsula of England. It was very much this type of setting which first drew the attention of another best-seller writer, Hammond Innes, like Winston Graham, a writer noted for the meticulousness of his research. In later years Innes has been famous for such novels as *Golden Soak*, for which he went to Australia to get the right atmosphere, *Campbell's Kingdom*, necessitating a similar visit to Canada, *The Angry Mountain*, researched in Norway – and of course *The Wreck of the Mary Deare*, based on his own experience of ocean sailing.

At the beginning of his career, Hammond Innes chose somewhere nearer home for his research, namely the St Just and Pendeen area of West Cornwall. Both *Killer Mine* and *Wreckers Must Breathe*, two of his early novels, were set in Cornwall, and in them this gifted narrative writer made full use of the knowledge he gained of the strange composite background of the elemental and the man-made (in this case the mines). In *Killer Mine*, for instance, there is a gripping description of the narrator following a suspect down into one of the mines.

> I stopped the gig at the main adit level and with my hand cupped over my torch so that it showed only a glimmer of red light I hurried down the gallery. The air was very still. No wind blew up from the sea. There was no sound of waves. The only sound was the drip of water. The quiet of the place magnified the sound. The drip of water and the stillness both seemed merged. It was as though night had seeped down into the galleries and the mine slept. The adit seemed longer than when I had come down it with Captain Mannack. I was almost running. I was afraid I had missed the old man. But when I reached the bend that brought me in sight of the bottom of the shaft he used, there was his lamp glowing yellow against the walls of the gallery. I stopped then. The old man was going down the gallery towards the sea. A ghostly glimmer of moonlight filtered down into the gallery as I went past the shaft by which he had descended. Glancing ahead of me I could see the ladders snaking up over the dripping rock walls.

In page after page like that Hammond Innes recreates for us an aspect of the Land's End area not so familiar as that above ground – the subterranean yet living underworld of the mines.

I sat there shivering and listening to the sound of water.
Perhaps daylight would show a gleam of light on the sea
water below. If not ... That didn't bear thinking about.
Nobody knew I was down here. I could stay here and rot.
And then suddenly I sat up. I thought I heard a voice, very
faint and distant. It was like a woman's voice. I listened,
but it did not come back again. I sat back. It was possible to
imagine all sorts of sounds in the dripping of the water. I
thought of the stories old tinners had told, stories of goblins
working underground, of the spirit of Gathon and sudden
flares and lights. 'Wherever there do be a lode of tin, thee's
sure to hear strange noises,' I remember one grisled old
miner saying. But they never spoke of a woman's voice ...

Just how tempting the Cornish scene, and indeed the
underlying atmosphere, must be for a novelist can be judged
from Hammond Innes' opening paragraph of his second
Cornish novel, *Wreckers Must Breathe*:

Cornwall is a wrecker's coast. But when I left for my
holiday I thought of the wrecker as a picturesque ruffian of
several centuries ago who lured ships to their destruction
with false beacons and waded out into angry seas to knife
the crew and unload the cargo as the vessel broke up. I did
not think of Cornwall as being still a wrecker's coast, and I
knew nothing of the modern wreckers I was to find havened
beneath the shadow of those grim cliffs.

Who could fail to read on after such an opening? More than
most writers, one might say, the author of adventure stories
can be understood if he turns instinctively to a turbulent world
like West Cornwall. And yet the more sensitive ones, like
Hammond Innes, respond as well to the other side of the coin.

I reached the top of the cliffs and paused for a moment to
look down on the calm leaden sea that heaved gently
against the rock-bound coast. The cry of the gulls was balm
to the turmoil of my thoughts. That high screaming cry had

always been synonymous with holidays to me, for from my earliest childhood I had always spent them on rocky coastland. There was peace here and quiet. I looked back at the little group of cottages huddling down the valley to the cove. It was satisfying to think that whatever happened this coast and the cottage would remain to bring peace of mind to those who lived on and to other generations.

A popular novelist of recent years who unlike Hammond Innes has completely buried his roots in Cornwall is Frank Baker, author of the best-selling *Miss Hargreaves* and a string of Cornish novels like *The Twisted Tree*, *Embers* and *The Downs so Free*. Early in his career when he took the plunge and gave up his job as a London clerk he went to live in a lonely cottage out at Kenidzhak Valley, Cape Cornwall.

At last I came to the gate and swung it aside. Down came the smell of stock, sensuously opening out to me in the spring flowering of the hillside. The warm moisture of the flower-filled night surged into me and drew me also deep into its living centre. I was an operative part now of all this, I said, as I climbed the last bit of steep path past the almost invisible beds of bulb flowers. I paused by the well listening to the blackbird singing wildly from the stone hedge at the bottom, an outpouring of ecstatic song which touched the strings of my heart and called out to music there. The wind blew from the west ...

The wind always blows from the west at that end of Cornwall and in many of his other Cornish novels Frank Baker has expertly captured this strange flavour. More than most 'furriner' writers he has seeped himself in the legendary forces of Cornwall so that he is forever bringing us up with a start: and most of what he has written about has to do with Land's End. Read, for instance, *Embers*, a beautifully composed study of characters around the Penzance area, in which the background cloth is not allowed to dominate some very vivid characterisation.

After living at Cape Cornwall Frank Baker went for a while 'up country' to Mevagissey, but since then he has spent most of his time first at St Hilary, close to the church of his friend Bernard Walke, where for a time he was organist, and more recently at Porthleven on the shores of Mount's Bay. It was here he wrote a recent book, *The Call of Cornwall*, which reflects a deep and personally felt understanding of what it means to live near the end of the land.

In Penwith, as each day comes to what we call an 'end', the last of the sun is seen from this Island of England. Here it seems possible to move down into the intangible horizon, with the sun; slowly to sink into the substance of the ever changing yet always unchanged motion of the sea. If the fall of the west is certain, so is the rise in the east. Yet in the fall lies the essence of man. And in the horn of plenty, the land of strangers, I was to discover the full truth of this.

When the darkness came and the valley was black so that even the thin line between land and sky could not be discovered, I realised for the first time that I was alone in a world that needed me to help sustain it. In London I had been no more than a cog in a clatter of machinery: in Leadenhall, my heart had become as lead. Here, the slaughtering sun forced me to consider my darkness and through it see a glimpse of undefiled light. In Cornwall this light may suddenly be seen in its full glory. But there will be days of dense mist in which the whole world is lost, and this is what I had recollected from my London desk.

It is a mistake to think of Cornwall as an escapist's paradise; and if one seeks escape there it will not be to an easy home, but to an external world of unsparing grandeur wherein a combination of forces can appear to be in conflict – sea against cliff, cliff against sky, trees thrashed double and stunted by devouring winds. Yet on a closer examination this can all be seen as a unity of forces, an energy of harmony. In Cornwall, the music of the spheres sounds through the linked architecture of its megalithic structure.

It is from Frank Baker, in another book of essays, *I Follow But Myself*, that we have this rather delightful record of a visit to Cape Cornwall of the famous literary critic and publisher's reader, Edward Garnett, who had told George Manning Sanders that he fancied a brief holiday in some remote 'place in the west'. Knowing about Frank Baker's ambitions to become a professional writer, George Manning Sanders told Garnett about this delightful little cottage in the Kenidzhak Valley where he would be well looked after ... meantime warning Frank on no account to 'let the writing cat out of the bag', but to let Garnett think he had discovered a budding new writer.

Garnett duly arrived with his secretary, Miss Heath. The weather was vile all the week. Frank Baker found himself marvelling at the vigour with which both his visitors went off on long walking expeditions, Garnett somehow propelling 'that large clumsy body of his along the rock slush of the Cornish lanes'. In the evenings the guests would sit around the dinner table.

The manner of Edward's after-dinner talk, consecrated by long habit, was thus. Once he had got into the mainstream of his thesis, which would of course be literary, he liked to pause at the semi colon of a sentence, reach for the bottle in an absent manner, hold a silence by the slow movement of the bottle towards the rim of the glass and then *before* he poured the wine, wind up his long phrases. Not until he had finished and it was apparent that he now awaited any comment would he offer a glass of wine to one of the company. It was a most impressive technique and it gave clear warning that any interruption of his long flowing vocal cadences was out of the question. He had to reach the pagal cadence and then the glass might be tilted and offered. One would listen to him almost as to an unfamiliar symphony unwinding its exposition and watch him as one would a conductor as the movements of the hands, bringing bottle and glass together, coincided with the semi colon

pause. And, of course, during the pause he would puff,
expelling air as though with it came thoughts too obvious
to be shaped into words: better lost.

Unfortunately for Frank Baker on the first occasion he forgot
to take the cork out of Edward Garnett's bottle so that just
when the great man was in full spate about such matters as
the lamentable works of the late Hall Caine and the opinions
of that redoubtable female, Mrs Elinor Glyn, and what Henry
James said to Conrad when they were arguing about reality
and art – just at the all important moment when he came to
tilt the bottle, no wine emerged! Despite this cardinal sin
Garnett, true to his reputation for shrewd appraisal, went on
to encourage the young writer – for, of course, it didn't take
him long to guess the truth of the matter – and in later life
helped Baker to find a publisher for his Cornish novels, *The
Twisted Tree*, of which reviewer Peter Quennel wrote: 'This
novel might have been written by the ghost of D.H. Lawrence
seated on the grave of Mary Webb.'

Mary Webb on Cornwall might have made interesting
reading but as far as I know she never visited the country. D.H.
Lawrence is another tale altogether. From a purely literary
point of view few periods in the history of the Land's End
peninsula have been more interesting than events at Zennor
during the years of the First World War and just after. This
small and remote country village and its surroundings seemed
to act almost like a magnet upon a formidable range of well-
known writers – among them D.H. Lawrence, Katherine
Mansfield, J. Middleton Murry, Dorothy Richardson,
Virginia Woolf, J.D. Beresford, Havelock Ellis, Saxon Sydney-
Turner and Peter Heseltine. As I said earlier, Zennor is a
remarkable place, an almost text-book picturesque village
nestling near the cove with a stunning backcloth of vast
moorland hills and the great ocean itself stretching away
northward in greeny-blue profusion to the very horizon. Small
wonder perhaps that, to take a minor figure first, Peter
Heseltine was prompted to write in a letter to his friend the
folk song expert Cecil Gray:

I am living now in a little wooden house on the highest part of the moor that separates the two seas, north and south – between Zennor and Penzance. All round, on all sides, nothing but open moorland and rock-strewn hills, mostly crowned with marvellous Druid temples. Without leaving the house I can see the sun rise at five in the morning and watch it sink at night into the sea. The sky never grows dark; the darkness seems rather to come welling out of the earth like a dye, infusing into every shape and form, every twig and every stone, a keen intense blackness. In the twilight bushes, walls, roofs, and the line of the hills all seem to become rigid and sharp against the sky, like dark blades, while the upper air remains clear and bright and the sky becomes more and more luminous as the blue deepens to a marvellous purple setting for the first star. The hollows and lower slopes of the hills are covered with a dazzling profusion of gorse and blackthorn – I have never seen such blazing masses of gorse. Tiny lizards dart about among the violets on the sunny banks and splendid gold and black adders often cross one's path on the moors.

The other day, looking down from the cliffs into a clear green sea pool I caught sight of a lovely young seal gambolling under the water. Up here on the moor all the birds and beasts come so near one, not suspecting any human presence. Foxes lollop leisurely along the road, bunnies hardly take the trouble to hop out of the way when one walks by. A chorus of larks makes the air ring all day long and there are cuckoos innumerable, piping from far and near with delightful variations of pitch and interval – sometimes two sing exactly together on different notes! And on the edge of the pond near by an assembly of huge gulls holds colloquy. I wish you would come and live hereabouts for a bit. There is an extraordinary fascination about this little remote end of Cornwall.

Indeed there was and in 1916 it sets its mark indelibly upon the burning consciousness of a man destined to be regarded as one of the great English novelists of this century, D.H.

Lawrence, who with his new, German wife, Frieda, was anxious to find somewhere peaceful and far from war-haunted London. And so:

'We go to Cornwall on Thursday. There is the beginning.'

Most of Lawrence's life seems to have consisted of fresh beginnings, usually of a geographical as well as spiritual nature, and Cornwall was to be no exception to the pattern: ecstasy, doubt, disillusion. First the Lawrences went to stay at Porthcothan on the north coast where they had been offered the loan of a cottage belonging to fellow novelist J.D. Beresford. Before long the chance rose to move further west to Zennor, 'a most beautiful place a tiny village nestling under high shaggy moorhills a big sweep of lovely sea beyond, such lovely sea, lovelier than the Mediterranean – five miles from St Ives and seven miles from Penzance.'

Even before Lawrence had actually settled himself and Frieda and their few belongings into Higher Tregerthen he began rhapsodising about it in a flurry of letters to his close friends the writer Middleton Murry and Katherine Mansfield, a New Zealand novelist and short story writer.

What we have found is a two-roomed cottage, one room up and one down, with a long scullery, but the rooms are *big* and *light* and the rent won't be more than four shillings. It isn't furnished, but with our present goods we need so little. The place is rather splendid. It is just under the moors on the edge of a few rough stony fields that go to the sea. It is quite alone, a little colony.

There are two blocks of buildings, all alone, a farm five minutes below. One block has three cottages that have been knocked into one and the end room upstairs made into a tower room; so it is a long cottage with three doors and a funny little tower at one end. The other block is at right angles and is two tiny cottages. But it is all sound, done up, dry-floored and light. I shall certainly take the little cottage.

What I hope is that one day you will take the long house with the tower and put a bit of furniture in it: and that Peter Heseltine will have one room in your long cottage;

and that somebody else will have the second cottage; that
we are like a little monastery; that Emma is in your kitchen
and we all eat together in the dining room of your cottage,
at least lunch and dinner; that we share expenses. The rent
will be little, the position and all is *perfectly lovely*. Katherine
will have the tower room with big windows and pannelled
walls (now done in black and white stripes, broad, and
terracotta roof) and Jack would have the study below, you
two would have the *very charming* bedroom over the kitchen
and pantry. The tower room is not accessible save from
Jack's study.

There is a little grassy terrace outside and at the back the
moor tumbles down, great enormous grey boulders and
gorse. It would be *so splendid* if it could come off! such a
lovely place: our Rananim.

I have quoted that letter at some length because it reveals the
almost hypnotic way in which Lawrence would set out to
persuade people to do what he wanted: and indeed, following
even more enthusiastic letters, the Murrys announced they
would soon be coming down. Meantime we find Lawrence
reflecting enthusiastically:

I like Cornwall very much. It is not England. It is bare and
dark and elemental, Tristan's land. I lie looking down at a
cove where the waves come white under a low, black
headland, which slopes up in bare green-brown, bare and
sad under a level sky. It is old, Celtic, pre-Christian ... The
house is a big, low, grey, well-to-do farm place, with all the
windows looking over a round of grass, and between the
stone gate pillars down a little tamarisky lane, at a cove of
the sea, where the waves are always coming in past jutty
black rocks. It is a cove like Tristan sailed into, from
Lyonesse – just the same. It belongs to 2000 years back –
that pre-Arthurian Celtic flicker of being which
disappeared so entirely. The landscape is bare yellow-green
and brown, dropping always down to black rocks and a

torn sea. All is desolate and forsaken, not linked up. But I
like it ...

Like so many other writers featured in this book Lawrence
was intrigued by the unique qualities of the West Cornwall
landscape and his comments are full of vivid descriptions of
gorse flickering with flowers, foxgloves and heather, all the
marvellous light of hills and the sea, fields with lambs skipping
and hopping, seagulls fighting with ravens and always this
strong elemental sense of the past, of King Arthur and
Tristan. It is not England, he says emphatically and goes on to
marvel at the magnificence of the Cornish scenery, the sea
breaking against the rocks 'like the first craggy breaking of
dawn in the world, such a comfort after all this whirlwind of
dust and grit and dirty paper of a modern Europe'.

Yet Lawrence being Lawrence, influenced though he was
by the physical setting, could not avoid turning his
penetrating imagination upon the Cornish people as well. At
first there was a ready sympathy: he found in them a rare sort
of natural flowering gentleness which appealed greatly. Then,
as so often in his life, he changed his mind abruptly.

I don't like people here. They ought to be living in the
darkness and warmth and passionateness of the blood,
sudden, incalculable. Whereas they are like insects gone
cold, living only for money, *for dirt*. They are all afraid –
that's why they are common. But I don't really understand
them. Only I know this, I have never in my life come across
such inertly selfish people. The Cornish have had a harsh
unprotected life, and in order to survive they have had to
withdraw into their shells – thus often seeming to an
outsider self-centred.

What probably upset Lawrence was the typical inbred
Cornish suspiciousness of all 'furriners' – an attitude only too
easy to understand in view of their past history, for like all
Celtic races the Cornish have known brutal and unjustified
oppression. Perhaps in time Lawrence may have reversed his

opinions again, but in fact he developed quite a hysteria in the matter, sneering that previously he had regarded the French peasants as vile but the Cornish were even worse, having no being at all. 'The only thing to do is to use them strictly as servants, inferiors, for they have the souls of slaves ... the barbarian conquerers were wisest really. There are many people, like insects, who await extermination.'

All this seems the more ridiculous when it is realised that during his stay at Zennor Lawrence became friendly with many of his neighbours, particularly the Hocking family who owned Tregerthen farm just down the lane. Indeed Christmas 1919 saw the two Hocking brothers, William and Stanley, and their sisters Mabel and Mary, all sitting at the round table in the upper room of the tower cottage with Lawrence proclaiming grandly, 'Everyone here shall be equal tonight'. After dinner Stanley played his accordion and everyone sang together – a cosy enough picture.

The fact was that, coming as he did himself from a strong working class background in Nottinghamshire, Lawrence had many things in common with a local hard-working group of people. He himself has often been described as living frugally, spending hours cleaning round the house, most efficiently running his own vegetable garden, mending furniture and generally excelling at domestic tasks. One visitor to Tregerthen described the 'little spotless sunny house' as having the most beautiful simplicity imaginable.

There is another aspect to Lawrence's feelings about the Cornish as ambivalent as so many of his other relationships – his persistent philosophising about the need for a kind of blood friendship with the elder Hocking, William Henry. Apparently William was a restless man, at odds with the head of the family, his mother, and so almost inevitably he turned to Lawrence as some kind of saviour. Of course Lawrence was delighted, exclaiming: 'There is something manly and independent about him and something truly Celtic, an unknown something non-Christian, non-European, but strangely beautiful and fair in spirit, unselfish.' When later on he came to write his novel *Kangaroo*, Lawrence gives this portrait of his relationship with William Henry.

> Somers stayed above all day, leading or picking, or resting,
> talking in the intervals with John Thomas who loved a half-
> philosophical, mystical talking about the sun, and the
> moon, the mysterious powers of the moon at night, and the
> mysterious change in man with the change of season, and
> the mysterious effects of sex on a man. So they talked, lying
> in the bracken or on the heather as they waited for the
> wain. And the farmer, in a non-mental way, understood,
> understood even more than Somers ...

According to Catherine Carswell, one of many writer friends
of the Lawrences who stayed for a period at Higher
Tregerthen, William Henry was a working man and a Celt
with a subtly pagan face, the kind of man born in the shadow
of Druidical stones, yet English, too, and must surely have had at
least some sort of wordless understanding of the ancient rites
about which Lawrence became obsessed during his stay in
Cornwall. There have been suggestions that some sort of
homosexual relationship took place between the two men. It is
certainly interesting that another famous novelist who spent
years in the Land's End region, Compton Mackenzie, quotes
Lawrence as once remarking to him: 'I believe that the nearest
I've ever come to perfect love was with a young coal-miner
when I was sixteen.' But in all probability Lawrence was
merely dreaming of some mystical kind of comradeship
between men – the sort of philosphy expressed by Walt
Whitman, one of Lawrence's heroes. At any rate in due course
the friendship between Lawrence and his Cornish neighbour
was broken off abruptly (by Lawrence, in some offence) when
the farmer married a local girl, Mary Quick.

Meantime Lawrence had become much more involved in
his more immediate intellectual relationships with the Murrys
who by now had actually braved the journey down from
London and were installed in the cottage next door. Looking
back and knowing the temperaments of the characters
concerned, it would be folly to imagine that such a scheme as

Lawrence envisaged, his Rananim, could ever have worked. Yet the beginning sounded hopeful to judge by this friendly comment from Frieda Lawrence.

> I see Katherine and Murry arriving on a cart, high up on all the goods and chattels, coming down the lane to Regerthen. Like an emigrant Katherine looked. I loved her little jackets, chiefly the one that was black and gold like bees ... I can remember days of complete harmony between the Murrys and us, Katherine coming to our cottage so thrilled at my foxgloves, tall in the window seat.

It is from Frieda that we get what little detail there seems to be of any source of harmony at Higher Tregerthen. Unlike her husband she was not particularly interested in achieving some kind of dreamy Rananim – she was simply rather glad to have some feminine company if only to relieve the tension of life with Lawrence. Although at least ten years older than Katherine, in later life Frieda remembered how the two of them had great times doing things together, like making pot pourri with dried rose leaves and herbs and spices or painting wooden boxes and having delicious female walks and talks. And how Katherine could talk!

> She had a Dickensish kind of way of giving small events a funny twist, and sharp and quick she pounced on anything funny that happened and gave you a swift look, the rest of her face innocent so that often I had a hard time not to laugh and be rude. If I had to describe her in one word I would chose the word exquisite. She was exquisite in her person; soft, shiny, brown hair and delicately grained skin, not tall and not small and not thin nor stout, just right. When we went bathing I thought her pretty as a statuette.

In these days when of course the Higher Tregerthen complex has been considerably altered, particularly Katherine's Tower, now modernised and recently for sale at £30,000, it is rather touching to reflect that perhaps somewhere on those

wild moors such eminent spirits still linger. Fortunately we
have more than ghostly records, for Lawrence wrote
continually in his letters and journals during that period, both
about the personal relationship with the Murrys and about his
own writing: at the time he was working on what was to be
one of his most notorious novels, *Women in Love* (some of his
novels are patently based on the Cornish background, and
upon the two couples, Lawrence and Frieda, Murry and
Katherine).

In fact Cornwall has a great deal to do with *Women in Love*
for it encouraged Lawrence to manage to ignore the outside
world, to withdraw into this more pastoral world, 'Here one
sits, as in a crow's nest, out of it all.' The purity of nature,
Cornish nature, permeates Lawrence's approach to the
writing of the novel, and he describes himself sitting with his
back against a boulder, a few yards above the houses, below
the gorse yellow and the sea blue:

'It is very still, no sound but the birds and the wind among
the stones.'

While the novel went well, the dream of Rananim was soon
shattered. There were several reasons for this. For one thing
whereas the physical nature of the Cornish landscape
obviously had an immediately favourable impact upon
Lawrence the effect upon Katherine was quite opposite. It is
difficult here not to feel sympathy, for the poor woman was
already on the way to an early death from consumption, and
her magical tower turned out to be something of a nightmare
most unsuitable for one in her condition.

Today I can't see a yard, thick mist and rain and a tearing
wind. Everything is faintly damp. The floor of the Tower is
studded with Cornish pitchers catching the drops. Except
for my little maid (whose ankles I can *hear* stumping about
in the kitchen) I am alone, for Murry and Lawrence have
plunged off to St Ives with rucksacks on their backs and
Frieda is in her cottage. I feel as though I have drifted out to
sea and would never be seen again. This house is like a ship
left high and dry. There is the same hollow feeling …

Then again both Katherine and Murry must have found very upsetting the incredible and violent exchanges that took place between Lawrence and Frieda. Here is one of them described in a letter from Katherine to the painter Koteliansky:

> I felt like Alice between the Cook and the Duchess. Saucepans and frying pans hurtled through the air. They ordered each other out of the house – and the atmosphere of a *hate* between them was so dreadful that I could not stand it: I had to run home. Lawrence came to dinner with us the same evening but Frieda would not come. He sat down and said: 'I'll cut her throat if she comes near this table'. After dinner she walked up and down outside the house in the dusk and suddenly, *dread*fully, Lawrence rushed at her and began to beat her. They ran up and down out on the road, scuffling, Frieda screamed for Murry and for me – but Lawrence never said a word. He kept his eyes on her and *beat* her. Finally she ran into our kitchen shouting: 'Protect me! Save me!'
>
> I shall never forget Lawrence, how he stood back on his heels and swung his arm forward. He was quite green with fury. Then when he was tired he sat down, collapsed, and she, sobbing and crying, sat down too. None of us said a word. I felt so horrified I felt that in the silence we might all die – die simply from horror. Lawrence could scarcely breathe. After a long time I felt: 'Well, it has happened. Now it is over for ever.'

Despite that vivid account Katherine is too perceptive not to observe that the next day Frieda stays in bed and Lawrence waits on her and takes up her meals, and she concludes that in fact Frieda actually thrived on these excitements. Well, she, Katherine, could not bear the falsity of it all and from then on she was determined that she and Murry should get away which they did by finding a cottage thirty miles away over at Mylor near Falmouth, on the south coast. Katherine's final bleak comment on her period at Zennor: 'It is not really a nice place. It is so full of huge stones and I feel I don't belong to anybody here.' While neither Murry or Katherine seem to have been particularly drawn to Cornwall nevertheless their experience at Zennor obviously had a profound if harsh effect on their lives.

As for the Lawrences, their time at Zennor too was coming to an end – though it was to happen in a much more dramatic fashion. It was still wartime, and in fact the height of the desperate period when the western approaches were beleagured by packs of German U-boats, and Cornwall was classified as a coastal defence zone. Several ships were sunk off the coast between Land's End and St Ives, and inevitably – what with Frieda having German nationality, not to mention her tactless habit of singing German songs loudly every night – some of the locals started spreading malicious rumours that Higher Tregerthen was a centre for spying. Later in the summer as many more ships were sunk more rumours were spread. One day while the Lawrences were out the cottage of Higher Tregerthen was searched by the military who took away letters, diaries, even manuscripts. The next day the police arrived and read out an order obliging the Lawrences to leave Cornwall within three days; to report to the police 24 hours after finding a new residence; and to stay out of Class 2 prohibited areas (one third of England, including all coastal regions).

Despite this shock Lawrence could not bring himself to feel that it meant leaving Zennor forever. He made up a great fire of his old manuscripts but otherwise decided to leave the house as it was, the books on the shelves, to take away only personal belongings. For he was determined to come back. As he later wrote in *Kangaroo*:

Until he had made up his mind to this he felt paralysed. He loved the place so much. Ever since the conscription suspense had begun he had said to himself when he walked up the wild little road from his cottage to the moor: shall I see the foxgloves come out? If only I can stay till the foxgloves come out. Then it was the heather – would he see the heather? And then the primroses in the hollow down to the sea: the tufts and tufts of primroses, where the fox stood and looked at him. Lately however he had begun to feel secure, as if he had sunk some of himself into the earth there, and were rooted for ever. His very soul seemed to have sunk into that Cornwall, that wild place under the moors. And now he must tear himself out.

Sadly Lawrence never made that return journey. In the years ahead other places drew him – France, Italy, Australia, Mexico. Probably only in the last however, did he ever feel quite so close to the elemental as he did in West Cornwall and in particular that 'splendid place on the edge of a few rough stone fields that go down to the sea.'

By a strange twist of fate not only was Virginia Woolf frequently in the St Ives and Zennor areas at much the same period as the Lawrences and the Murrys, there was even a moment when a correspondence took place between the two lady novelists about the possibility of Virginia buying Tregerthen Cottage. Although Katherine had not liked the place when she stayed there, she seemed to take a kinder view some time after the event and wrote encouraging her older friend to buy the cottage. 'Immediately you get there you will feel as free as air,' she wrote enthusiastically. There seems to be no final record about the transaction, but in one of her letters Katherine wrote: 'It is indeed thrilling to think that Higher Tregerthen is yours.' – and she went on to look forward extravagantly to visits she would never make, advising Virginia that white and purple veronicas would grow well in the cottage garden. Perhaps in the end Virginia's more cautious husband Leonard stepped in and put a stop to any romantic notions she might have harboured – and of course rightly so, for somehow it is difficult to see the fastidious Virginia buried at Higher Tregerthen, cut off from all literary contacts. Probably for her the best solution was what happened: a series of holidays down at Zennor, staying at the Tinner's Arms or in nearby cottages.

Unlike Lawrence, Virginia Woolf was no stranger to the area. Before she was born her father, the critic Leslie Stephen,

had made many walking tours of Cornwall and finally bought
a holiday home in St Ives, Talland House, an elegant
Victorian building standing high up with views over St Ives to
the bay. Here, in marvellous surroundings within sound of the
sea and sight of Godrevy Lighthouse standing white and
shining on the Gwithian horizon, Virginia Woolf spent
seemingly endless childhood holidays, playing cricket with her
sister Vanessa and her brothers Thoby and Adrian, not to
mention six-year-old Rupert Brooke, or walking with her
father up to the top of Trencrom, or swimming and sailing, or
just watching the tide come in and go out. Sometimes the
children would climb the granite rocks to Clodgy Point or up
to the little fisherman's chapel on top of the Island – there
was really no end to the outings. Boat trips, too, with her
father, across the wide bay, stopping for some mackerel
fishing on the way back – outings which left vivid and useful
imprints on the novelist's mind, as later reflected in *Jacob's
Room*:

> The mainland, not so very far off – you could see clefts in
> the cliffs, white cottages, smoke going up – were an
> extraordinary look of calm, of sunny peace, as if wisdom
> and piety had descended upon the dwellers there. Now a
> cry sounded, as of a man calling pilchards in a main street.
> It wore an extraordinary look of piety and peace almost as if
> the end of the world had come and cabbage fields and stone
> walls, and coastguard stations and above all, the white sand
> bays, with the waves breaking unseen by anyone, rose to
> heaven in a kind of ecstasy.

Although later on, particularly after her marriage to Leonard
Woolf, the novelist spent more time in London and her home
at Sussex, she always remained avid to return to the
mysterious land of her youth, renting cottages usually at
Zennor. At such times, inevitably, Vanessa would receive
letters like this one:

> It is pitiable to think that you are bothering about pictures

and no doubt leaving your umbrella on Haverstock Hill while I am watching two seals basking in the sea at Gurnard's Head. This is no poetic licence. There they were, with their beautifully split tails and dog-shaped heads rolling over and diving like two naked dark brown old gentlemen. Two minutes before a viper started up under my feet. The smell of the gorse which is all in bloom and precisely like a Cornish picture against a purple sea is like – I don't really know what. We are on the cliffs quite by ourselves, nothing but gorse between us and the sea, and when I have done this letter we are going to take our books and roll up in a hollow over the sea and there watch the spray and the bees and the peacock butterflies.

The same ecstatic note was struck in a later letter to the critic, Saxon Sydney-Turner:

We are between Gurnard's Head and Zennor. I see the nose of the Gurnard from my window. We step out into the June sunshine past mounds of newly sprung gorse, bright yellow and smelling of nuts, over a grey stone wall, on along a track scattered with granite to a cliff beneath which is the sea, of the consistency of innumerable plover's eggs where they turn grey-green, semi-transparent. However when the waves curl over they are here like emeralds, and then the spray at the top is blown back like a mane – an odd simile doubtless, but rather a good one. Here we lie resting though L. pretends to write an article for the *Encyclopedia* about 'Co-operation'. The truth is we can't do anything but watch the sea – especially as the seals may bob up, first looking like dogs, then like naked old men with tridents for tails. I'm not sure that the beauty of the country isn't really its granite hills and walls and houses, and not the sea. Of course it's very pleasant to come across the sea spread out at the bottom, blue, with purple stains on it, and here a sailing ship, there a red steamer. But last night, walking through Zennor, the granite was – amazing is the only thing to say. I suppose, half transparent, with the green hill behind it, the granite road curving up and up. All the village dogs were waiting outside the church, and the strange Cornish singing inside, so unlike the English. I often think about the Phoenicians and the Druids and how I was a nice little girl here and ran along the top of the stone walls ...

Virginia Woolf's profound feeling for Cornwall can be traced in several of her books, apart from letters, and in particular in *To The Lighthouse*: there is a passage where Mrs Ramsay is describing watching, hypnotised, the beam of the lighthouse stroking the floor of the bedroom in the night 'as if it were stroking with its silver fingers some sealed vessel in her brain whose bursting would flood her with delight; she had known happiness, exquisite happiness, intense happiness.' And in the same novel is an evocative description of Mrs Ramsay looking out upon the bay and seeing across the great plateful of blue water 'the hoary lighthouse, distant, austere, in the midst; and on the right, so far as the eye could see, fading and falling, in soft low pleats, the green sand dunes with the wild glowing grasses on them which always seemed to be running away into some moon country uninhabited of men ...'

It was with *To the Lighthouse* that Virginia Woolf won the Hawthornden prize. It is very much an intellectual's book and yet constantly in the descriptive passages, even if put into people's mouths as conversation pieces, the images and influences of Cornwall are forever breathing through. Like every other major writer who has ever lived in Cornwall Virginia Woolf was never able to forget the extraordinary impact of this wild and elemental country:

'The romance of Cornwall has once again overcome me. I find one lapses into a particular mood of absolute enjoyment which takes me back into my childhood,' she wrote to her sister, going on to add: 'How I wish you were here – as only the Cornish see its stupendous merits.'

Long after her father had sold Talland House, and indeed after her own marriage to Leonard Woolf, Virginia kept returning to Cornwall for holidays – often staying at Zennor. It was out of these visits, one feels, that her ideas began to crystallise for *The Waves*, in which there is the pregnant sentence: 'In the beginning there was the nursery with windows opening on to a garden and beyond that the sea.' She is always haunted by the sea, by water – ironically, since eventually she drowned herself – and in *The Waves*, just as in *To The Lighthouse* there can be no doubt but that St Ives and its surroundings are the material she is using. 'But for a moment I had sat on the turf somewhere high above the flow of the sea and the sound of the woods, had seen the house, the waves breaking.' It was as if she could not keep away from all her past memories. Many many years after those childhood times she was able to remember exactly the flowers in the garden at Talland House; the purple passions, the evening primroses, the pampas grasses and 'the red hot pokers like braziers of clear burning coal, between which the blue waters of the bay looked bluer than ever.'

Unlike that distinguished contemporary novelist, Daphne du Maurier, Virginia Woolf never settled in the county she loved so much, but there can be little doubt that she was very considerably influenced by its 'stupendous merits'. Lovers of West Cornwall will find more perception and truth in many of her fleeting phrases often in pages of loquacious guide books. After all, as she once commented blithely: 'I always feel that I am the original owner of Cornwall and everyone else a newcomer!'

Virginia Woolf and Katherine Mansfield were regarded as two of the outstanding women writers in England during the early part of this century. By a final irony the St Ives area to which they both at one time gravitated was also (from 1912 onwards) a home for another leading woman novelist who, in the words of her biographer, John Rosenberg, in *The Genius They Forgot*, 'changed the course of the modern novel, only to become one of the great unread'. Indeed Mr Rosenberg goes further and makes the claim that Dorothy Richardson was the real creator of the 'stream of consciousness method' (a phrase which she detested) and the immediate precursor not only of Virginia Woolf and Katherine Mansfield but of James Joyce and *Ulysses*. Even Virginia Woolf, though later more grudging about her predecessor, did in an early review of one of the first novels, *Revolving Lights*, admit that here was the first novelist to create a method and a language for expressing the feminine consciousness.

As it happened, Dorothy Richardson came to Cornwall by much the same route as D.H. Lawrence – that is to say, through the good offices of the novelist J.D. Beresford. At the time she was struggling to write *Pointed Roofs*, the first section of her great work *Pilgrimage*, and already mixing in Bloomsbury circles – having had a tempestuous love affair with H.G. Wells, by whom she had a child who died. The Beresfords had a house in St Ives, and near it a cottage converted from an old ruined chapel. Now they pressed Dorothy to come down and stay with them. Living was cheaper in Cornwall than in London: if she wished, she could live in the chapel and write undisturbed. The chapel was said to be haunted but they didn't think that would worry her.

Dorothy Richardson accepted the invitation and, in her fortieth year, went to live in St Ives. While there she met Beresford's friend, Hugh Walpole, and she and the other two novelists would take long walks along the Cornish cliffs. Altogether things looked promising; living in the chapel suited her and she worked well, commenting: 'Suddenly the world had dropped away. But never had humanity been so close. Everything took on a terrific intensity.' Certainly she worked hard, but at first things went badly: she felt her novel was just like every other novel and she was determined to achieve a new approach – and indeed, after many fresh starts, so she did.

Pointed Roofs was turned down by the first publisher it was sent to and Dorothy Richardson promptly hid it away in a trunk but Beresford persuaded her to let him send it to Duckworth's, whose reader, Edward Garnett, liked it and classifying it as 'feminine impressionism' recommended publication. When the book appeared it sold moderately but had a *succes d'éstime* and was widely reviewed by those who mattered – including Virginia Woolf who said, 'She has invented, or if she has not invented, developed and applied to her own uses a sentence which we might call the psychological sentence of the feminine gender.'

From then on the rest of Dorothy Richardson's long life was devoted to writing the remarkable sequence of thirteen novels eventually brought together under the overall title of *Pilgrimage*, and for a great deal of this time she lived and worked in Cornwall. She also got married to an artist, Alan Odle, who suffered from both tuberculosis and alchoholism, which added to life's difficulties (he was also about fifteen years younger than Dorothy). Soon after the marriage, in August 1917, the couple moved down to Cornwall, wandering around that wild coast enjoying their 'days out':

> When we first ferried across we wandered blissfully, quite lost, over the dunes and on and on, finally getting ourselves back only to find we had missed the last ferry. There we stood vainly shouting towards a quay empty of people all of whom were making merry up in the town. At last just as we were meditating a night in that large hollow on the dune, partly overhung by crumbling moss-grown sand, we saw, coming across the water, a small rowing boat. Our eager yells produced a moving oar and soon there landed a wild looking being, skeletal, with fierce red hair and gold earrings, who had seen us from the top of the cliff. A knight errant whom we had to compel to acceptance of our combined cash.

Days like this gave them both a sense of escape from all the pressures of London and as Alan was beginning to like Cornwall too they decided to find a place of their own. This was Rose Cottage:

> a genuine labourer's cottage, one square window in the front room, with a huge kitchen for warmth and cooking (and smoke) and a cupboard in the same room for coal. No water nearer than the pump in the road outside the strip of long grassed uncultivated garden. Outside sanitation ... it must have been the gloomiest little hole imaginable, but

this was never noticed, and each of us having for so long been an inhabitant of one room we felt *palatial*.

During her period in St Ives Dorothy Richardson met D.H. Lawrence, and liked him. She described Lawrence as

> an electric shadow in a room ... he is always himself. His style is himself and never a deliberately contrived effect. He does make his presentation of experience current, as is all experience if presented as a result of a sufficient intensity of concentration.

Soon after the war period Dorothy Richardson and her husband moved from St Ives further up the Cornish coast to Padstow, renting various bungalows and cottages around Trevene and it was up here that she wrote the next five volumes of her *magnum opus*. By now though her earnings were small her fame had spread all over the world, thus gaining her friendships with many distinguished writers such as John Cowper Powys, Ford Madox Ford, Gertrude Stein, 'Bryher' and Ernest Hemingway. In particular, John Cowper Powys became a devoted friend, writing, 'Deep my dear is the feeling and hero worship that I have in my old heart for you. It has been one of the great things in my life.' Powys it was who thought it a scandal that such a great writer was so ignored and he compared her to Wordsworth, Blake, Nietzsche and Schopenhauer in a list of 'the great Neglected'.

In fact Dorothy Richardson outlived nearly all her literary contemporaries and even her much younger husband (who died in 1948). She herself went on living at Trevene, but often paying visits to St Ives and that area where she had many friends. She eventually died in June 1957, in her eighty-fourth year, yet another example of a truly great figure in our literature who had found in Cornwall both a haven and an inspiration.

V

Through The Poet's Eye

Sometimes a prominent contemporary literary figure who has been drawn to Cornwall has finally been enticed that little bit further, to the Scilly Isles. Such a person is John Fowles, author of *The Collector, The Magus, The French Lieutenant's Woman* and other notable novels, whose fascination with islands led him to produce two books about the Scillies, *Shipwreck* and *Islands*. However, as is often the case, even in passing through, so to speak, a perceptive writer can illuminate our own scene. Here, for instance, is the opening paragraph of *Islands*:

The wise visitor to the Scillies does not drive straight to Penzance and board a helicopter or a ship but finds time, so long as the weather is clear and visibility good, to go out first to Land's End. And there they float, an eternal stone armada of over a hundred ships, aloofly anchored off England; mute, enticing, forever just out of reach. The effect is best later in the day, when they lie in the westering sun's path more like optical illusions, mirages, than a certain reality.

At Land's End you already stand on territory haunted by much earlier mankind. Their menhirs and quoits and stone lines brood on the moors and in the granite walled fields; and even today the Scillies can in certain lights lose the name we now call them and re-become the Hesperidean Islands of the Blest; Avalon, Lyonesse, Glasinnis, the Land of the Shades; regain all the labels that countless centuries of Celtic folklore and myth have attached to them. Their

burial places are scattered all over the present islands, and
so densely in places that one suspects the Scillies must have
been the ultimate Forest Lawn of megalithic Britain,
though internment there would not have been an ambition
of only the dying. The spirits of the dead could not cross
water, and the living may well have cherished that thirty
mile *cordon sanitaire* between themselves and their ancestors.
Whatever the reason, the islands hold an astounding
concentration of nearly one fifth of all such tombs in
England and Wales – or more than Cornwall, which is
already rich in them.

John Fowles goes on to expound the theory of the lost land of
Lyonesse and suggests that the legend arises from the fact that
the ancient Celtic inhabitants of West Cornwall had contacts
with a much more advanced culture whose ships would have
appeared out of the south-west even though their homeland
lay in quite another direction. He has the Phoenicians in
mind, and quotes an account given by Diodorus Siculus,
writing in the first century BC.

The inhabitants of that part of Britain which is called
Balerium (Land's End) are very fond of strangers, and from
their intercourse with foreign merchants, are civilised in
their manner of life. They prepare the tin, working very
carefully the earth in which it is produced. The ground is
rocky, but it contains earth veins, the produce of which is
ground down, smelted and purified. They beat the metal
into masses shaped like astralgi (dice) and carry it to a
certain island lying off Britain called Ictis (St Michael's
Mount).

From his studies John Fowles goes on to explain that tin
smelting pits dated back to 300 BC have been found near
Land's End, at St Just, and that ' in short, though positive
proof is lacking, there does seem strong circumstantial
evidence to suggest that mysterious strangers were descending
on the extreme south-west of Britain, and regularly, from

Homer's time and possibly even before it. I believe myself that this is where the northern version of the Atlantis corpus of legends springs from.'

If we now stay in the Land's End region and explore the narrow winding lanes around St Buryan and Porthcurno, in this literary survey of Land's End, we come across one of the least expected figures – Dylan Thomas. The fact is that just before the last war the man destined in posterity's view perhaps to be regarded as Britain's greatest poet of his time was tempted down west. It happened – as these things so often happened in Dylan Thomas's untidy life – through what might politely be called force of circumstances, or rather lack of them. Some of Dylan's friends in London were becoming alarmed at his alcoholism, and knowing he had practically no money persuaded a mutual friend, Wyn Henderson, the musician and typographer, to write to the poet offering free board and lodging at her little cottage at Polgigga, a tiny hamlet just outside Porthcurno on the road to Land's End. Perhaps surprisingly Dylan allowed himself to be persuaded:

How nice of you to purr about me after dinner, two fed, sleek cats rubbing against the table-legs, and thinking about a scrubby Welshman with a three-weeks-accumulated hangover and a heart full of love and nerves full of alcohol, moping over his papers in a mortgaged villa in an upper-class professional row (next to the coroner's house) facing another row (less upper) and a disused tennis court. It was a lovely rolling letter, out of the depths of dinner, and a winey mantle of love hung over it, and thank you a lot ...

As your mascot and a very welcome guest, I'd love to come to Cornwall more than anything else: it sounds just what I want it to be, and I can write poems and stories about campire sextons deflowering their daughters with tiny scythes, and draw rude little pictures of three-balled clergymen, and to go pubs and walks with you. It's all too lovely to be good; and I'd enjoy it so much. I'm coming to town in about a fortnight; I've got to meet a few publishers and try to get money from them as I haven't any, and, I believe, to read some poems over the wireless. That won't take long: the publishers will (probably) pretend to be deaf, and the wireless will break down. If you are gone by then, chugging into Cornwall, shall I follow you and will you meet me, lost with beer in my belly and straws in my hair? And if you haven't chugged away, but are still rampaging in Bloomsbury (or wherever you rampage mostly) we can go together, can't we? And that will be nicer still.

In the spring of 1936 Dylan was installed at Miss Henderson's cottage at Polgigga, near Porthcurno, hardly more than two miles from Land's End itself. It would seem a romantic if somewhat bizarre setting for the ebullient Thomas, but his most immediate concern was with the (for him) rather primitive domestic background. He complained that he was living in a cottage in a field with a garden full of ferrets and bees – 'every time you go to the garden lavatory you are in danger of being stung or bitten'. Apparently he found his hostess rather trying, for she was inclined to talk about his ego over breakfast, and her conversation was rather too liberally sprinkled with phrases about narcissist fixation and homosexual transference. Nevertheless, the one good thing was that he was doing 'lots and lots of work': stories, poems and – ironically, in view of his location deep inside the brooding, mysterious Kingdom of Kernow – a travel book on Wales.

Work apart, we are not left in much doubt about Dylan Thomas's initial reaction to Cornwall. In a long letter from the Polgigga address to his great friend Vernon Watkins, another well-known Welsh poet, he declared:

Now in a hundred ways I wish I hadn't come away: I'm full of nostalgia and a frightful cold; here the out of doors is very beautiful but it's a strange country to me, all scenery and landscape, and I'd rather the bound slope of a suburban hill, the Elms, the Acacia, Rookery Nook, Curlew Avenue, to all these miles of green fields and flowery cliffs and dull

sea going on and on, and cows lying down and down. I'm
not a country-man; I stand for, if anything, the aspidistra,
the provincial drive, the morning cafe, the evening pub; I'd
like to believe in the wide open spaces as the wrapping
around walls, the windy boredom between house and
house, hotel and cinema, bookshop and Tube station: man
made his houses to keep the world and the weather out,
making his own weathery world inside; that's the trouble
with the country, there's too much public world between
private ones. And living in your own private four-walled
world as exclusively as possible isn't escapism, I'm sure; it
isn't the Ivory Tower, and even if it were, you secluded in
your Tower know and learn more of the world outside than
the outsidesman who is mixed up so personally and
inextricably with the mud and the unlovely people – (sorry
old Christian) – and the four bloody muddy winds.

During the rest of that year Thomas moved backwards and
forwards between Cornwall and Swansea and London, and it
was during this period that he first met his wife-to-be, Caitlin
Macnamara. At the beginning of the summer of 1937 they
both came down to Cornwall, living for a time at the Lobster
Pot, a hotel on the water's edge at Mousehole, near Penzance.
It is interesting that Thomas was drawn to Mousehole, a
small fishing village which he once described as 'the loveliest
village in England' ... for, geographically and structurally,
with its doll-like cottages rising up in steep tiers on the
hillside, Mousehole could well have been a setting for *Under
Milk Wood*. Who knows but that one day in the future some
erudite literary scholar may prove that Thomas used something of his knowledge of Mousehole in writing the play?

It was from Mousehole, anyway, that Thomas set out on
one of the shortest, yet most decisive, journeys of his life – to
the registrar's office at Penzance, where he and Caitlin were
married on 12th July 1937, 'with no money, no prospect of
money, no attendant friends or relatives, and in complete
happiness ... We've been meaning to from the first day we
met, and now we are free and glad.' To his friend Vernon

Watkins Dylan added: 'I think you'll like Caitlin very much, she looks like the princess on top of a Christmas tree, or like a stage Wendy; but, for God's sake, don't tell her that.'

Soon the Welsh bridegroom and his Irish bride were installed in a typical Cornish 'artist's' home, a studio above the fish market in Newlyn, where seagulls flew in for breakfast. Although it was to be a short stay, the Thomases enlivened it considerably with many boisterous gatherings in the Newlyn pubs, followed by parties up at the studio. Quite a few literary friends from London were persuaded to come down on visits – notably Rayner Heppenstall, one of Dylan's favourite drinking companions in London. Heppenstall stayed quite a while, and in fact used Cornwall as a setting for his best known novel, *Blaze of Noon*, about a blind masseur.

Like many other writers and artists before and after him Dylan Thomas must have found the social life of the Cornish art colonies a pleasant one. Pub-wise, Newlyn and Mousehole and St Ives could offer almost as much variety as London or Wales. And, on his own admission, he worked very well down in Cornwall. Nevertheless neither he or Caitlin really seemed to feel settled in their studio where the gulls flew in for breakfast: and by the end of that same year they had left Cornwall and moved nearer to London, settling in Caitlin's mother's home at Ringwood, Hampshire.

Henceforth, the poet's tragically short life was to take him far from Cornwall – to Italy and to America, where he eventually died during a lecture tour. He never lived in Cornwall again, though no doubt he retained a sentimental nostalgia for 'the loveliest village in England', as well as a lifelong memory of that momentous visit to the little registrar's office in Penzance. Yet, looking back, it is difficult not to feel that a place like Cornwall was bound to have a striking impact on a poet of Dylan Thomas's stature – even if an antagonistic one ... and I dare say that if one was to search assiduously through the poems written at the time, or even later, it would be possible to trace quite a few images and lines commemorating that fleeting contact between Dylan Thomas and 'a strange country to me'.

Sometimes in surveying the literary scene of Land's End the choice of material becomes positively embarrassing. Before embarking on this book I felt reasonably sure that it would encompass quite a large number of important literary figures but I had no idea how many. Of course, some have been temporary visitors and in cases where the visits were brief and the authors not especially interesting, pressure of space has seemed to justify their exclusion. When the same problem arises in regard to authors who have actually lived in the district the problem becomes more of a headache ... despite all my efforts to encompass as wide a field as possible, invariably there are quite a few names that can only be touched on fleetingly.

Wallace Nichols, for example. Born in Birmingham in 1899 he came to Cornwall for health reasons in 1934 and stayed there until he died three decades later – spending his last years (after his wife's death) living in a house in the grounds of Nancealverne, Penzance, the former home of Judge Scobell Armstrong. Wallace Nichols was one of the last of the Georgian poets and it was as a poet and writer of verse plays that he held himself in highest regard. *The Guardian* commented on his *Laodice*, 'It is written in blank verse that at times is almost Shakespearean,' the *New Chronicle* declared 'much of his verse has a lyric beauty as pure as it is memorable,' the *Scotsman* reviewed his book of selected lyrical poems as 'works to be compared with Keats' 'Nightingale' but, to modern readers, more satisfying' and everyone enthused about his dramatic morality in two acts, *The Boy from Egypt*, based on the legend that Christ as a boy came to Cornwall with his uncle, Joseph of Arimathea.

Poetry, however, was only one string to Nichols' creative bow and he was both amazingly prolific and remarkably versatile as an author. In all he produced more than sixty books which included historical romances, boys' adventures, essays and detective novels (one critic picked out his series of short stories featuring Sollius, the Roman slave detective, as 'the best since Sherlock Holmes'). He was also a renowned authority on speaking verse, having taught Laurence Olivier,

Edith Evans and John Gielgud among others. Yet he must remain in the shadows of this survey though it is certainly worth quoting some remarks he once made about the local land's influence on his work:

> Cornwall's aura of the past certainly stimulates the writer's imagination. If you go through Madron Village towards the open moor beyond you are on the edge of prehistoric country, filled with the memories and memorials of a lost race ... one feels near the beginning of things on a Cornish moor. For my part the triangle formed by lines drawn from Madron to Morvah, thence to Zennor and back to Madron is the most wildly magical area of West Cornwall, and I would willingly surrender any of the coves and beaches for its astringent beauty.

Charles Simpson – a distinguished painter who spent many decades living and working in a large Georgian house in the centre of Penzance and made a useful contribution to the literature of Land's End with autobiographical books in which he attempted to analyse the Cornish landscape and its influence on painters and creative artists generally – is another figure deserving more attention than is possible here. He was always fond of recalling that moment of the day, the hour of twilight, when the Cornish hills would seem to loom hugely above the sea and the tokens of men dead or alive were alike swallowed up – as day departed so the power of the granite almost seemed to rouse up to watch the approach of night.

> The area of Cornwall which impresses the mind most strongly with the peculiar quality of brooding, of vengeful menace, of the unrest and terror added by man, of cataclysmic events beyond his sphere, lies between the cliffs at Land's End and the narrow watershed some few miles nearer sunrise. Here the waves along two opposing coastlines appear to strive which shall be first to wear down the resistance of the rocks and make an island of the westward hills. It is possible to gaze from sea to sea and

listen almost at the same moment to waves breaking on either side, to hear the roar of surf swirling round the black cliffs to the north and long rolls sweeping up the southern shore, and thus in imagination to conceive the peninsula as an entity aloof from the mainland. Fantasies of the past surge round its people. The northern cliffs frown upon the sea, an unbroken barrier of rock, grey as the Jackdaw's mantle, sombre as the raven's wing. Dull tones of thunder cloud and rain-storm find their match on the highlands, darkening the bracken to green of a leaden hue in summer, to swarthy smouldering red in autumn ... The very sunlight is colder, bleaker, sadder than elsewhere. Those who wander on the moors enter the domain of fog ... the shades of some dawn that never breaks, some paler counterpart of night. Sunsets there are, and golden skies, but they seem ruled by a capricious power who wills the sun to shine half in eclipse. The land has a countenance whose smiles only intensify its gloom and if there is laughter on the hills it is hollow as the cackle of an aged man.

And again from Penzance comes a totally different concept of the Land's End area, in the words of two contemporary local authors, A.C. Todd and Peter Laws, in their book *Industrial Archaeology of Cornwall*. After pointing out that people who these days buy some remote cottage on a headland or in some valley winding down to the sea should realise that in the eighteenth and nineteenth centuries West Cornwall was as industrialised as the Midlands, the authors describe their experience of standing amid the chaos of Levant Mine, near St Just, in all its stark abandonment and realising the shattering challenge that faces the modern industrialist archaeologist.

As he sits among the wreckage somehow he has to visualise again the complex of buildings growing as they did before the eyes of those old engineers and craftsmen and then to try and visualise the natural landscape as it was *before* they occupied it and adapted it to their own needs. Equally the industrial archaeologist has an important contribution to make to what might be defined as the aesthetics of industry: engine houses that take on the appearance of Cornish chapels: granite stairways in mines that are as beautifully designed as any in a church tower; factories that were made to look like the coach houses of the gentry; chimney stacks that, for their mathematical precision of construction, bear comparison with the columns of a Roman temple; and crushing mills that one could easily mistake for part of a medieval monastery. There is all this and more for both the professional and the amateur archaeologist in Cornwall, where a single capstan in a cove below the mining town of Pendeen led to the discovery that some Cornishmen spent their days winning tin from the darkness a thousand feet or so 'below grass' and their nights in searching for fish, choosing to name their cluster of cottages, St Peter's Row'.

Then, around the Penzance area alone, there are many more names – J.C. Tregarthen, author of *Wild Land's End, The Life of a Badger*, etc.; John Dryden Hosken, the poet; Peter Pool, authority on the Cornish language ... However lest it be thought that Penzance is the only portion of the Land's End peninsula to have an embarrassment of writers, let us move across the Penwith hills through that strange mid-way village of Nancledra and we are reminded at once that here resided for thirty years one of the genuine eccentrics among contemporary writers in Cornwall, now a septuagenarian but still going strong, Arthur Caddick, often referred to as the Poet Laureate of West Cornwall (partly on the strength of a stream of weekly odes and sonnets he has contributed for many years to the local *Cornishman*). Originally with a wife and six children to support, Caddick lived in the same small cottage from 1946 onwards, dividing his time initially between writing poetry and humorous autobiographical pieces and performing the bizarre duties that went with the acquisition of the cottage – attending to the well-being of the nearby Cornwall Electric Power Sub Station.

One of the old-fashioned type of actor poets who liked nothing better than to declaim his poems in public places, in his younger days Caddick was often a familiar figure in St Ives, Penzance, Zennor, Gurnard's Head and other convivial centres. With his booming voice, his tall and angular frame, usually topped by a broad brimmed old trilby hat, he looked the epitome of the old Shakespearean actor-manager. Listening to him reading his poetry was often the best way of appreciating it, for above all Caddick was witty and humorous, but the fun came out best in the manner of reading. When regretfully I had to close down the first series of my literary magazine the *Cornish Review* in 1950 Caddick wrote me a delightful farewell poem – when miraculously we managed to restart the magazine in 1966 he was quick to supply a welcoming poem, 'The Second Launching':

Three cheers for Cap'un Baker and his craft,
The Resurrection-Man who piles his decks
With gallimaufries from the Cornish scene
And brings his poets little Celtic cheques!
What rich embroideries of Cornwall's life,
Lie ready for unloading in his hold,
The mine, the cove, the pilchard moon, the croft,
The wrestling of the modern with the old!

Despite those cheery good wishes once again the *Cornish Review* came to an untimely end, but not before we had published a wide range of excellent writings – among them several of Arthur Caddick's poems and some interesting extracts from a projected autobiography, *Laughter At Land's End*, full of richly comic passages of struggling life as a poor writer up on the Nancledra hills, with his strange part-time job:

I was summoned to emergency duty at any time of the day or night by a titanic alarm bell in our bedroom. 'Art thou poor, and hast thou golden slumbers?' The bell rattled like a machine gun and everything in the bedroom rattled with it as its thunderous tocsin shook the cottage, much as the hunchback's tolling shook the belfry of Notre Dame. I would dive at the bell out of dreams and switch it off. Then

I had to hare like hell over the croft to the Sub-Station and peer at a spectral array of dials until the hand of one of them revealed to me what had blown up and where. I then telephoned Control at Hayle Power Station and told them the worst ... then the gang of linesmen started their tour of inspection to find the fault. They would swarm up towering poles in darkness, often with a seventy mile an hour gale lashing rain into their faces, and might have to patrol and climb throughout the night, and then all the next day, to restore supply to Cornish homestead and factories and farmers and hotels, all the vast diversity of means by which the Cornish earn their living.

At other times Caddick had hilarious experiences with visits from friends like the alcoholic poet, the late John Gawsworth, or Sydney Graham from nearby Madron. Then there was his famous libel case where he sued the Ancient Company of Makers of Wood for damaging his reputation as a writer by forcing the *Cornish Review* to leave out a satirical poem. The case came to court, Caddick conducted his own prosecution and it ended with a settlement under which the Ancient Order agreed to commission Caddick to write them a new song in praise of their mead!

Nancledra, as Caddick has described it, is the first village on the Cucurrian, the red river, after it rises from Amalverow Downs on the slopes of Trendrine, near Buttermilk Hill. The source of the Cucurrian, springing from granite and crystalline rock, is hidden by furze and heath and bracken, and its watershed is a hill which is part of the majestic barricade which seals off the prehistoric interior of the last length of the Land's End peninsula before the Cornish earth dives abruptly into the Atlantic. The Cucurrian river winds down from Nancledra past Boskennal Mill then through Ludgvan Woods, in a deep granite chasm cut by the breaking of glaciers at the end of the Ice Age, and reaches the sea near Marazion.

Such a place has nurtured many writers in its time – once, for instance Sven Berlin, then better known as a sculptor, but subsequently to earn a deserved reputation as a novelist, lived in a granite cottage opposite the Engine Inn, at Cripplesease with his gypsy wife Juanita. Sven also had a studio on the Island at St Ives where he worked on his dramatic sculptures, but it was in his little cottage where he began his writings. He had a brilliant way of expressing a feeling for the Cornish seascape:

> The open coliseum of each little cove of sand or rock may be the theatre for any natural, supernatural or unnatural agent. The unending presence of the sea breathing ceaselessly over the shoulder of each hill, the rock charged with a thousand sunsets or carved by a hundred years of rain, the little trees loaded with berries growing away from the prevailing wind, offering crimson to green, the mind's incessant vertigo at the cliff edge, and the slow constructional flight of the seagull – these things in some way act as the charming of magicians and open up the deeper rooms of experience in man, making him aware of his being part of the natural universe, at the head of a great unseen procession of gods and devils, spectres and dragons, of being a channel for unknown and undefined forces, facing the mystery of life, awakening powers of perception which search beyond the frontiers of normal events.

That extract comes from Sven Berlin's book *Alfred Wallis*, about the old St Ives fisherman turned primitive painter, who at the age of seventy began painting in house paints on old pieces of cardboard, a flood of child-like efforts which today are on the walls of numerous art galleries all over the world (and now worth many thousands of pounds whereas poor Wallis was paid in shillings or ounces of tobacco!). Later Sven Berlin began writing fiction and produced what in my opinion is the best novel ever written about St Ives *The Dark Monarch* – alas, as is so often the case with the best things in life, it is banned and you will be lucky to find a copy. But try, because in its pages Berlin vividly brings to life the bizarre and fantastic flavour of life in an art colony. Unfortunately (for him!) too many of the richly colourful characters were identifiable with real people who, not surprisingly, took strong and legal objections. Nevertheless in future ages when personalities have passed on and can no longer be hurt this novel will be a valuable piece of documentation.

Altogether Sven Berlin is a most interesting example of a number of artists-turned-writers in contemporary West Cornwall, and he had some valuable observations to make. For instance it seemed to him that the terraced landscape of the little fishing towns and the geological nature of the rock at once became operative, along with 'the submarine cargo of shells, skulls, fish and plants,' in orientating one's vision back to the fundamental shapes of nature ... This added to the peculiar influence Cornwall had upon the unconscious mind of man brought into line once more the ancient forces of creation that have a close affiinity with the spirit of life. In such an environment about humanity penetrating its mechanical armour and seeing it once again as a dynamic part of the universal order governed by the mystery of God. And Sven Berlin went on to try and put his own experiences in Cornwall into words:

> When the sea gets into a leg I am carving what excitement there is! It goes charging through the whole of the stone and a man, as if by magic, is transformed into an ocean with rocks and tides, shells and caves – a sea-dragon. The whole galaxy of one's experience pours in upon him: one works in a kind of dream as though someone else is making the image. Is it not true that the doors of life, when open, release shapes and forces hidden inside us for ages? Be that as it may, there is no *reasonable* explanation of what happens. All I know is that it was Cornwall that helped to release and develop my ability to create something living out of stone.
>
> After a while I became so deeply rooted in the Cornish landscape that to go and carve in a city, in a forest, or among mountains would so alter my vision that it would probably be impossible to work for a considerable time.

Literary St Ives of recent times, not surprisingly, tends to have been dominated by the artists many of whom have proved impressively articulate. For several decades the art colony life was headed by Ben Nicholson, the abstract painter, and his wife Barbara Hepworth, the sculptor. Nicholson was the subject of a full length book by art historian J.P. Hodin, in which he is quoted as saying that the structure of Cornwall, where he lived from 1939 for several decades, suited him.

> Yesterday I began to paint the garden gate. As soon as my hand touches a brush my imagination begins to work. When I finished I went up to my studio and made a picture. Can you imagine the excitement which a line gives you when you draw it across a surface? It is like walking through the country from St Ives to Zennor.

That country from St Ives to Zennor also fascinated the late Peter Lanyon who once at my request made an imaginative attempt to capture in words what he felt about it as a painter, in an article in the *Cornish Review*:

> The Cornishman is not double-faced but multiple-faced, facets of character which add up to a sort of innocence. He is never still himself except in death, but all the conflicts which lead to a game of hide and seek between native and the so-called 'foreigner' are part of a process which constantly surfaces the most diverse and conflicting factors. The Cornishman is fond of private secrets. A solemn intercourse of native with native, often intimate, is mistaken for a gossiping and vicious moralizing. The bush telegraph which puts the GPO to shame is a part of this intimate revelation from native to native. The part of this game which is revealed to the unfortunate 'foreigner' is that part which concerns him alone, the rest is none of his business. Prayer is a strong force, and in the greatest days of revivalist services, in Wesleyan chapels, a poetic resolution was achieved. The loss of such inspiring services is as sad for Cornwall as the closing of the mines.

There is a main force which is centrifugal and centripetal, a giving out and a taking in. In extremes this means a complete trust and desire to give absolutely everything and a converse withdrawal, a returning to a protective native envelope. The eye is prospecting and adventurous, it has also an inward look. Perhaps these qualities are most often found in insular people, and perhaps Cornwall itself has for centuries been almost an island. The Cornishman will change according to basic rhythms which are suggested here and will make a good job a 'fitty' job as he says, not one just fit for purpose but a fitness within a rightness which is determined by his whole history and the nature of his country.

Peter Lanyon, tragically killed as a result of a gliding accident in 1966, went on to give this painter's eye view of the Penwith countryside:

From Wicca to Levant the coastline emerges out of carns and bracken and cultivated greenland, revealing on its varied faces a sea history and a land history of men within and without and a commerce of man with the weather. Here, in a small stretch of headland, cove and Atlantic adventure, the most distant histories are near the surface as if the final convulsion of rock upheaval and cold incision, setting in a violent sandwich of strata, had directed the hide and seek of Celtic pattern. A motor-boat in some solemn gaiety with insistent cough, searches out the exacted payment of ocean on land; the small ritual of business at the junction of rock and sea wall. On carns of Zennor, Hannibal and Galva, where giants may have hurled their googlies in mild recreation, an outline of earthwork makes evidence for a primitive brotherhood of man, of the great and small in life and death wherein animal joy and terror found resolution in the protective care of monolith and fort. Hereabouts, perhaps, the sun set westwards, shifting down the monolith to bury the light of primitive fire, and rose again in the hearts of men from the east. The saints were in Cornwall ...

From Levant to Wicca, an easterly direction, chimneys are crowned by brick flourish and the towers are lichen-covered, castellated and pinnacled. They rise upward out of the horizontal ground as if the thrust of stone had surfaced to the call of the native, given up its wealth to his endeavour, and been revealed by manufacture as an expression of inner intent. Invention leading to extension of native culture, made present in time a process of ancient developments. The craft and skill and meaning of the native journey are outward and revealed at the land surface.

To bring the world within the hand and make immediate the farthest shore, seamen set sail for the mistress of the sea. From storm and shipwreck the homing seaman returns with cargo, unloading on granite quays a wealth of image. What stories he tells, and in his sea soul gives to the land, remain outwardly in his artefacts, are revealed to generations by the face of man and the character of his seaborn gear. This process has been a source of man's struggle to make himself as outward and revealed as this place of granite. Here sea and land answer the deep roots of man and present him with a face ...

At Levant Mine, where tin and ocean meet, men fished for food after labour beneath the ocean bed. What is within the granite arms of harbour, sheltered from surface mood and ground sea is concerned with an intimate bobbing, the playful game of boat with mooring, a small outward exchange reflective of deep ocean movements. A happy commerce in granite embrace. But the centre and focus of lighthouse, port and parent are left alone as masts and sails, clumsy with their clawings, move out to their own aggressiveness. Man-engine and steam haulage pass contact to deep levels with man-baited rod and line. Where shifts go down and come up and ships in regular exchange remove themselves and return to parent, the resources of Cornwall are best displayed and landed. In every small and

intimate departure or arrival a wholeness of living is
revealed, and in commerce of man and granite and Atlantic
the transitory is made immediate, each facet being related
elementally to the next as aspect and image of a whole ...

Considering its position as a centre of artistic activity for
nearly a century St Ives seems to have produced surprisingly
few literary figures. At the beginning of the century there were
one or two minor novelists like 'Ranger Gull' (Guy Thorne)
and for a time just before the last war Havelock Ellis and his
wife lived at the Count House, Carbis Bay, where he wrote
studies of psychology and she an autobiography. Well-known
novelists like Hugh Walpole, living at Truro, J.D. Beresford,
at Porthcothan, Compton Mackenzie at Hayle, were frequent
visitors, often to be found in the Sloop, that snug pub on the
water's edge. But resident writers have been fewer. After the
war a Canadian novelist, Norman Levine, settled in the town,
and wrote a number of short stories with St Ives and its
surroundings as settings but when he came to try a novel
about the art colony life it suffered the same fate as Sven
Berlin's, having to be withdrawn in the face of several
threatened legal actions. Perhaps St Ives is a little too sensitive
to provide a safe field for the fiction writer – or perhaps, more
likely, truth there is often stronger than fiction!

There are, of course, exceptions. One old hand is Mary
Williams, a prolific romantic novelist who still lives at her
studio home at Westcott Quay, many of whose melodramatic
tales of Cornish life have been published not only in this
country but on a wide scale in America. Apart from her novels
she has an excellent feeling for ghostly stories, many of which
we published in the *Cornish Review*. Somehow Mary Williams
manages in a few phrases expertly to capture all that side of
Cornwall recollected in the old saying about 'ghosties and
ghoulies.'

It was late afternoon when I saw the village and the
yellowing autumn dusk was closing quietly round the
humped line of moorland hills so that the great Cromlech

became submerged – crouched into the shadows like some ancient beast taking its rest. There was no sound save the thin high crying of a gull from nearby and the rustle of dead leaves as I walked down the lane ... I realised suddenly how tired I was: and with the knowledge came a swift unexplainable depression: this was odd because one expects to be tired after a day's tramp over the Cornish moors. But I could not shake off the sensation. The nearer I drew to the village the stronger it became. The very silence grew sinister, charged with an evil that no words can adequately describe ...

Immediately one relaxes, knowing we are off on a rattling good tale of mystery and terror!

Another contemporary writer to make his mark with his short stories about St Ives – though he has since left the district – is Kenneth Moss. Perhaps one day he will write the eventual 'right' novel about St Ives, for he had some interesting feelings about the way the place has changed when he paid a return visit.

St Ives I did see again, and having done so I suddenly feel that I belong to an older generation as if I have jumped up the ladder – or perhaps I've been pushed. I feel *passé – démodé*. In the short time I've been away the whole place has changed. Behind my back, as it were. I don't mean physically. Physically the town looks almost exactly as it did the first time I ever saw it. What has changed is the population. And not the indigenous population, about whom I never knew very much anyway, but the population of expatriates. St Ives has always had a large population of refugees from England, and these are the ones who are different. I know they come and go, but over a period, surely? Not all at once, in one great exodus. It is as if some latter day Moses has suddenly led them out of the House of Bondage. Some Pied Piper has charmed them all away and replaced them with a younger and (or do I just imagine it?) more callow lot: I had the feeling of belonging to a past generation, a lost generation, the one that has 'passed over'.

This of course is only an impression, because I still saw many of the old faces and I suppose if I bothered to count them they probably outnumbered the new. But so many have gone that the town seems to have changed its character. There is a distinct impression of the old order having passed. I have seen the end of an era. When I call the roll of those who have gone it seems to me that St Ives has not only lost many people, it has lost quite a lot of talent, too. Will the newer inhabitants make it up again?

What is interesting about Kenneth Moss's observation is that it can be applied (and is) to many other centres of West Cornwall, particularly in relation to the literary or bohemian life with which this book is concerned. That is why I suggest he might have his finger on a good approach to writing a novel about a place like St Ives, for this is a perennial experience among all artists who come to live in Cornwall. The golden age has just ended ...

In St Ives it seems then that it is the non-fiction writers who have flourished. Notable among them has been the local historian, Cyril Noall, whose stream of painstakingly researched histories – of wrecks, of smuggling, of tin mining, culminating recently in the elaborate and profusely illustrated *The Book of St Ives* – will be of inestimable value to future scholars.

St Ives, too, was a main subject taken by Charles Henderson in his posthumously published *Essays in Cornish History* where he gives a fascinating picture of 'St Ia' in the old days. Henderson was typical, though perhaps the most outstanding, of a long line of Cornish historians to whom we must be grateful – many of them living down in the western end (he grew up in Hayle). Up to the time of his death he was assembling voluminous notes for a penultimate *History of Cornwall*, and there are now 16,000 ancient documents of his in the Museum of Truro, with many hundred transcripts by his hand. Dr A.L. Rowse has painted an endearing picture of Charles Henderson: 'People up and down Cornwall began to recognise the figure perched on a hedge to draw old church towers or bent to scrutinise a granite slab for traces of its early use.' In due course the University of South West appointed him to lecture about the towns and villages of Cornwall, and all his short life was devoted to mastering a knowledge of his county such as no one else could claim. It is impossible here to do justice to a remarkable man and scholar – his death at the early age of thirty-three was a sad loss.

As to the literary side of St Ives, then, the most interesting writing to emerge has remained books of the type I have quoted, the work of articulate artists like Sven Berlin. Another in this category was the world-famous potter, Bernard Leach, who spent more than fifty years of his life living in St Ives (he died there in 1979). His writings were nearly all about pottery, though he sometimes embarked on religious works based around his Baha'i faith, so that his comments on the West Cornwall scene have been limited. However, in *A Potter's Notebook* he commented interestingly on the local aspect of the pottery which he founded in St Ives in 1920 with the Japanese potter Hamada:

At the Leach Pottery, by accepting the Cornish motto of 'One for All and All for One' and by making the workshop a *we* job instead of an I job we appear to have solved our main economic problems as hand-workers in a machine age, and to have found out that it is still possible for a varied group of people to find and give real satisfaction because they believe in their work and in each other. To me the most surprising part of the experience is the realisation that – given a reasonable degree of unselfishness – divergence of aesthetic judgement has not wrecked this effort. When it comes to the appraisal of various attempts to put a handle on a jug, for example, right in line and volume and apt for purpose, unity of common assent is far less difficult to obtain than might have been expected.

The Shakespearean scholar F.E. Halliday was a close friend of Bernard Leach, and like him lived in one of the pleasant flats overlooking the huge surfing beach of Porthmeor. Here he wrote a scholarly and fascinating book about Sir Richard Carew – *A Cornish Chronicle* and also his *History of Cornwall*. In this, like so many others of the writers I have quoted in this book, he went out of his way to emphasise that in spite of all progress, or railway, motor car and even aeroplane, Cornwall remains all but an island, un-English, a foreign country, seaward and southward looking 'towards Namances and Bayona's hold' and beyond Spain to the Mediterranean, the ultimate source of Cornwall's ancient culture.

And in spite of foreign invasion that culture has not been altogether lost in the Celtic kingdom of lost causes and lost industries – for although their numbers continue to shrink there are still thirty times ten thousand Cornishmen, independent, clannish, parochial even, proud of their separate history symbolised by quoit, Saint, huer's hut and sky fingering mine-chimney. When therefore the visitor from the East crosses the Saltash Bridge he must remember he enters a country scarcely penetrated by the English until a few centuries ago, peopled by men whose origins are different from his, who not long since spoke a strange language. And as he travels back westward, back in geological time, he also travels back in the history of men ...

A hundred years ago Cornwall's hills were loud with miners but grass and bracken have covered their trackways and workings, and along the coast from Pendeen to Botallack stretch ruined mine buildings, massive as some deserted Roman city plunging sheer into the sea. Yet these are but recent monuments to the passing of man's achievment and centuries before the miners came, centuries before the Saints and the Romans, the land was peopled, perhaps more thickly than any other part of Britain, by the builders of hilltop citadels and promontory forts, of megalithic monuments, stone circles, menhirs and the chambered tombs of Land's End. And westward still beyond Land's End, beyond the legendary Lyonesse of

King Arthur, lie the Fortunate Isles, among whose sunken shores it may be that relics of even earlier men have perished.

Opposite St Ives across the bay lie the famous 'three miles of golden sands' of Hayle – and Hayle, as Daphne du Maurier has said, makes a good point of entry to the world of Penwith. Compton Mackenzie is perhaps the most famous writer associated with Hayle, but there have been one or two minor writers whose gifts have noticeably been uplifted by contact with the strange brooding aura of those endless dunes (which stretch as far as Gwithian, the place that fascinated Francis Kilvert in his time). Notable among these writers is a native of Hayle, Erma Harvey James, who in *Rose Quartz*, an extract from a novel, which I first published in the *Cornish Review*, gave this fascinating memory of her last childhood summer on the Hayle sands.

I found the vast stretch of sea and shore indescribably melancholy. And the miles of sand-dunes stretching as far as the red river which stained the sea crimson as though some monstrous creature had perished upstream in a torrent of blood. Perhaps it was simply that it was all too dream-like, verging on another reality. There was a tradition that it had once been all meadowland and that the sand had covered it in a night. Marram grass and sea couch grass had been planted to stabilise the shifting dunes, but there were still a few 'open' ones with shifting sand. Among the dunes were the remains of the old Dynamite Works where one day during the war an explosion had occurred which sent everyone within miles running in panic from their houses and had broken the windows of the church at St Ives on the other side of the bay. There was scarcely a family in Hayle who had not lost someone on that dreadful morning. Some of the ruins still stood among the languid waving grasses. And in a wild garden of bugloss and sea-holly doorways opened onto a voice and flights of granite steps led up into the empty air.

And then, once one had got to the beach there was, from my point of view, and in comparison to days at Wheal Alfred, so little to do. I could dig a hole in the sand and watch the water seep in from the sides, or I could dig a slightly deeper hole and bury one leg or an arm, but that didn't take long. The sand itself was very fine, sparkling with mica, and ran like the sand in an hour-glass and I would take some in my hands and let it run through my fingers, pretending it was time itself running out, and that the quicker I let it run the sooner the day would be over. Near the shore the sea was usually green. And the glassy green waves would foam up the beach, break, and then run out leaving the sands laced with salt streams. One day when I was playing at desert islands ('deranged by thirst') I tasted one of the streams and found it was fresh water. It appeared to flow from out of a mass of rock which sloped up the cliff, and when I climbed the slope I saw that it was coming from the floor of an underground passage which ran into the cliff. Here was an adventure.

In delicate prose Erma Harvey James recreated far-off life in Hayle when there used to be a belief among the local people that every year the river 'cried for a heart'. And through the long hot days she felt that they were quite simply and silently waiting for this to happen.

Every summer while we lived there someone was drowned at the mouth of the river. Sometimes it was a stranger who didn't know about the currents and the quicksands, but quite often it was someone local. Whoever they were, the cried for were always buried with great solemnity in the cemetery among the sand dunes at Phillack. Through the gap in the houses one could see the horse-drawn hearse and long procession of carriages, and faintly hear the sound of the hooves and wheels. On the day of the funeral which was always held on early closing day, the blinds of all the houses along the route were drawn from early morning until late in the afternoon when the hearse was sighted returning across the Black Road at a brisk trot. And yet the people seemed to have little belief in personal immortality. 'There 'tis,' they would say, wiping their eyes, 'Never see un no more. Never no more.'

VI

A Coastline for All Seasons

Among the writers to whom Land's End beckoned with an almost hypnotic appeal one of the best loved was Lady Vyvyan of that grand old house Trelowarren, near Helston. Sadly Lady Vyvyan died recently but she left behind her a formidable legacy of erudite books about Cornwall, about gardening, about her travels all over the world, written either under her original name of C.C. Rogers, or more latterly C.C. Vyvyan. In point of fact Lady Vyvyan was born in Australia but after marrying Colonel Sir Courtenay Vyvyan, member of a noted Cornish landowning family, she acquired a devotion to Cornwall surpassed by few natives. This emerges in such books as *Letters from a Cornish Garden*, *The Scilly Islands* and *The Old Place*: and in particular in some of her earlier volumes of essays, such as *Cornish Silhouettes*, in which she sets out to express just what Cornwall means to her. In Cornwall she points out the wildness never beckons you on and on with unfulfilled promises – quite the contrary, it is there all the time waiting to be shared.

The loneliness of Cornwall is a loneliness unchanged by the presence of men, its freedoms a freedom inexpressible by description or epitaph. You cannot say Cornwall is this, or that. You cannot describe it in a word or visualise it in a second. You may know the country from east to west and from sea to sea, but if you close your eyes and think about it no clear-cut image rises before you. In this quality of changefulness have we possibly surprised the secret of Cornwall's wild spirit – in this intimacy the essence of its

charm? Cornwall! I see a barren stretch of country where no
green things find a home; only sparse heather clumps have
gained foothold in the many coloured stones; pink and
gold, purple and green, all the colours of the rainbow are in
the mineral fragments at my feet and the magic of the
desert is in the colourings of those stone heaps that stand
against the sky, so near yet so remote of aspect. No sound of
busy engines now; those rough mine dumps show no trace
of human toil; even the chimney stacks silhouetted on the
horizon have a solitary beauty of their own. They stand
there, more suggestive of prehistoric ruins than of recent
activity, crumbling slowly, ivory coloured, the haunt of
raven and jackdaw ... there is a peculiar intimacy between
man and nature in this lonely land and a peculiar sense of
remoteness from things that hamper and restrain.

The farmers say nothing when you climb their gates or
cut across their fields. The carters are slow-moving and
barely more alert than the horses plodding at their side.
The scattered houses and villages do not stand up with
proud independence; they nestle into the ground in
comfortable fashion and the farm buildings and stone
fences look like natural features ... The country is open
because no high hills bar the horizon, yet mysterious
because so full of variegated nooks and changing aspects.
You are never far away from the waves rolling in endlessly
to that rock-bound shore. There is no restlessness or
movement, desire or discontent in the atmosphere; perhaps
there is little progress. Man has not brought every acre into
subjection. He has but settled in the wildness and left it to
grow all around him. He is no alien conqueror of the soil;
he has never left the land nor does he ever wish to leave it.
He can no more strike a false note than the trees can on the
granite boulders, half embedded in the earth.

Lady Vyvyan is one of a group of talented contemporary
women writers whose names will always remain especially
associated with Cornwall. Apart from herself and Daphne and
Angela du Maurier, there is the late Anne Treneer, author of

the delightful autobiography *Schoolhouse in the Wind* and *The Mercurial Chemist*, a study of Penzance's favourite son, Humphry Davy; Mary Butts, Ruth Manning Sanders, Hilda Quick, Molly Mortimer and, in particular, Rosalie Glyn Grylls, widow of the late Sir Geoffrey Mander, and author of 'Reflections on the Cornish' one of the best essays I ever published in the *Cornish Review*, in which she vividly captured the nature of these people who are forever haunted by the past. First indeed she quotes approvingly George Meredith's claim that the past is literally always at the elbow of a pure Celt. That past, he said, lost neither face nor voice behind the shroud, nor were the passions of the flesh, nor is the animate soul, wanting to it. Other races might forfeit infancy, youth and manhood in their progression to the wisdom age may bestow but these the Cornish had each stage always alive, quick at a word, a scent, a sound to conjure up scenes in spirit and in flame.

Although she lives now in Wightwick Manor, near Wolverhampton, one of England's stately homes (famous for its William Morris tapestries) Rosalie Glyn Grylls remains an active author, having produced several biographies. But it is for her shrewd analysis of the Cornish character that she belongs here.

What is more remarkable than Celtic truth is Celtic imagination; its paucity and impotence. Where are the poets and artists and composers of the first rank? Where, even, the interpreters of the Arts or the Connoisseurs? The Cornish are not artistic – nor are good artists – but they are not artists either. Their quick response to stimulus is not imagination, not the 'creative spirit' in action. Seeing piskies on the downs or knockers in the mines is nothing to do with imagination; with the Cornish it isn't even imaginativeness, but simply reaction to a sensitized soil. There lacks the capacity to make that final effort for delivery which clothes the word with flesh. The men of science have come nearest to having it; Humphry Davy, John Couch Adams, Jonathan Couch, and inventors like

Trevithick or Trengrouse. They have been able to take the leap that brings light across the gulf. It is part of the Celtic paradox that it should be so.

No people gambols less in a Celtic twilight. In the Celtic heyday twilight was an awful hour that presaged the darkness. It only became picturesque to a gas-lit generation when Pan petered out in Kensington Gardens. Where does it go, then, all the colour? The warm tones of manner, the light and shade of speech? The colour goes into the personality. Almost one might say it is enough for the Cornish to be Cornish; but not quite, for they have a full measure of Celtic discontent. The energy that makes for colourfulness goes into the business of living – always a hard one in Cornwall: the fervour into congregational worship – into a personal relationship with omnipotence, not into embellishing its dwelling-place; the enterprise into seeking fortunes afield ... A forgotten larger part of the population of Cornwall is overseas – pioneers in a great trek to minefields and ranches that has, characteristically seldom been recorded, for with all their ability at dressing the window the Cornish are not good at selling their wares. They come home when they can (and always send back gifts generously), and to die when they can, but it is a small proportion over which to erect perpetual angels of nostalgia. The granite in those that go away is more typical of the back bone of the country than the lichen that remains.

Sometimes a writer's association with Cornwall has become magnified by legends – this has happened, perhaps understandably, in the case of Aleister Crowley, 'The Great Beast' to quote the title of John Symonds' biography. Always a controversial figure during his lifetime, Crowley's reputation has continued to hover in the background ever since; a supposed practitioner of black magic, organiser of ancient druidic rites, blood spilling and so forth. He was, as it happened, a very hard-working and prolific writer of many books, and it is evident from the philosophies expressed that he was indeed deeply immersed in all kinds of ancient rituals. It is popularly supposed that Crowley was a frequent visitor to Cornwall and that though he had little to say about the county in his books, he must inevitably have carried on some of his curious practices while down here. Certainly I have heard stories about his conducting dozens of black masses at St Buryan Church and there is a popular rumour of him and a group of disciples dancing naked round the stone circle at Tregasea – not to mention druidic ceremonies up on remote carns, like Trencrom.

Whatever contacts Crowley had with West Cornwall seem to have been centred on the Newlyn, Lamorna, Mousehole area in the main. It was at the Lobster Pot, Mousehole where he stayed in 1938 during the only visit of which there is an actual record. From there he spent his days climbing the rocks walking along the coast, sun-bathing and sea-bathing, enjoying convivial evenings with friends at the Lobster Pot or the Mousehole pub, The Ship, or at the nearby pubs of Paul and Newlyn or The Wink at Lamorna. Possibly during some of this time the Great Beast ventured upon some occult practices but if he did so there is no record in his voluminous diaries – instead there are references to his other main interest, sexual exploits – 'Wooed Greta on the cliffs'. By all accounts, Crowley had quite a magnetic personality and was very attractive to women and often held them in bondage. Here is a description of him by a contemporary West Cornwall writer, Ithell Colquhoun:

I saw a squarely built man of medium height who appeared to be in his middle sixties. His skin was the colour and texture of parchment, and thinning grey hair was scraped across the crown of his head; glasses (rimless or steel-rimmed) straddled his nose; features in no way remarkable were set in a long heavy face. People seem to have been puzzled by his eyes having variously described them as black, brown, yellow, green and the colour of horn; to me they seemed none of these, but a transparent grey, like water. My guess is that they were the kind of eyes whose

pupil dilates and contracts with unusual rapidity, so that
the tone and colour of the cornea appears with changing
conditions, psychological, as well as physical, depending as
much on mood as on intensity of light ... There was no
dramatic aura of evil surrounding the man; if I had not
known who he was I should have assessed him as a not too
prosperous country squire, with a kink or two. Nevertheless
he certainly made an impression on me.

Ithell Colquhoun herself is an author with a long-standing
Cornish connection, having lived in Lamorna and now nearby
Paul for several decades. Originally a painter, indeed still a
painter with frequent exhibitions both here and abroad, in
recent years she has turned to writing as a means of evoking
most vividly what she sees and hears about Cornwall, the
scenery of a gaunt and uniquely attractive county, its people,
mythology and Celtic legends. After an earlier book about
Ireland, *The Crying of the Wind*, she produced one of the best
'insider' books on Cornwall, *Living Stones*, essays on such
diverse aspects of Cornish life as the traces of King Arthur,
Padstow's 'Obby 'Orse, Helston Fair, the Gorsedd, the
woodcutters of Lamorna and local witchcraft. In this book
Ithell Colquhoun pursues a theory which has become
increasingly popular among writers in West Cornwall.

If the whole of Cornwall possesses a definite peninsula
character this is increased as one reaches the near island of
West Penwith. Even today it is almost completely divided
from the rest of Cornwall by water if you take into account
the streams that link the Hayle estuary with the marshes
west of Marazion. Here a low-lying valley runs almost from
the north coast to the south; but further east the watershed
between the two coastal areas is actually narrower, being
no more than the space dividing the source of the brook at
Pengersick and that of the stream flowing past St Germoe's
church to join, ultimately the Hayle river ... West Penwith
may once have been, owing to changes in the relation of
land to water, an even closer approximation to an island

than it is today. To go further east, that inlet of the River Fal leading to Tregony was a navigable waterway used within living memory by ships of fair size even though today it is no more than a brook. Judging by the number of prehistoric cemeteries it contains Penwith might well be called 'hungry for the burial of natives' – a common condition of islands.

Ithell Colquhoun is most penetrating when she seeks to interpret, indeed, the living stones of Cornwall. The life of the region, she asserts, depends ultimately on its geological substratum for this sets up a chain reaction which passes, determining their character in turn through its streams and wells, its vegetation and the animal life which feeds on this, and finally through the type of human being attracted to live there. In a profound sense also the structure of its rocks gives rise to the psychic life of the land; granite, serpentine, slate, sandstone, limestone, chalk and the rest have each their special personality dependent upon the age in which they were laid down, each being co-existent with a special phase of the earth spirit's manifestation. West Penwith is made up of granite, one of the world's oldest rocks a substance associated instinctively with endurance and flexibility – interestingly enough the basic elements of the Celtic and therefore Cornish character. Ithell Colquhoun suggests the fundamental fact about Cornwall is that if for some reason you do not like granite then you will literally never be happy there – if however like many people you experience an instinctive response to a granite boulder hung with grey and golden lichen, especially if set high on some lonely moor or above a raging sea far below, then you are likely to feel at home.

Ithell Colquhoun, John Michel, Charles Simpson, Sven Berlin, are typical of a group of largely contemporary writers on West Cornwall whose works deal very directly with the influence of the land mass itself upon people and their lives and thoughts. This same aspect has also been treated by writers in other fields – most notably, the poets. There are today a large number of well-known poets, both Cornish born and settlers, who have written most vividly about the Land's End peninsula. Take, for instance, the Redruth poet D.M. Thomas, editor of that fine anthology *The Granite Kingdom*, much of whose own work has been centred on the western tip – as for instance this poem on Botallack:

Needles flake off into the blue air. Listen.
In the August silence, on the bare cliff-path, you can fling
a stone and it will not break the silence, but you can hear
the wedges and drills or erosion hammering
in a silence that is uproar, beneath the wrecking Brissons.
The sea might ring to a finger today. Bone-china.
Without the drama of weathers, no flowers or trees
to mask time with recurrence, time's raw nerve
shows through here like an outcrop of tin. A peace
that is the acceptance of defeat reigns. Miners

trekkd this vertical, nerves tempered granite;
at their heads, candles – defeat – disaster – dowsed,
to stride out under the sea as courageous,
poor in all but tall tales the ocean housed,
as their Methodist Christ walked out upon it.

Botallack locks against too strong a force;
blue-framed, nettled engine-house, cliff-set. The logan stone
of me is here. Bal-maidens spalling ere
for bread feared not the plunge. Why should I alone
stride ahead of the flood, on a white sea-horse?

Down in these spirit heights, if the guttering
candles failed, kind –
ly light amidst the encircling gloom, one man
guided them unfailingly through blackwaters. He was blind.
In the country of the blind, that man was king.

Few pieces have captured in such a compressed way so much

of the mysteriousness of a county that remains a strange mixture of elemental and human (man-made) activities. One that does come to mind, however, is also from the pen of a famous living Cornish poet, Charles Causley, of Launceston. These stanzas from his poem entitled simply 'Cornwall' seem somehow to capture a sense of slumbering hidden strength that lies waiting to be brought to the surface, most especially around Land's End.

> One day, friend and stranger,
> The granite beast will rise
> Rubbing the salt sea from his hundred eyes
> Sleeping no longer.
>
> In the running river he will observe the tree
> Forgoing the slow signature of summer
> And like Caliban he will stumble and clamour
> Crying 'I am free! I am free!'
>
> Night bares her silver wounds in the sky
> And flees from the shouting sun.
> O monster! What spear, what rock gun
> Shall storm the fortress of your clear eyes?
>
> Your teeth sharpened by many gliding waters,
> Lying awash in the snarling tide
> How long, how long must you wait to ride
> Swagged with thunder on lovers and traitors?
>
> Cast off your coloured stone ropes, signal the tourney!
> And to the bells of many drowned chapels
> Sail away, monster, leaving only ripples
> Written in water to tell of your journey.

Other Cornish poets like Dr A.L. Rowse and Jack Clemo have been equally moved by the elemental side of their home land, but their work has been mostly concerned with 'up-country' though always the sea and land make their influence felt.

Behold the gulled and gorsed rocks,
Afternoon honey in keen wind sunlight
Myself on an ultimate stone
A water world about me
All movement and wind and sea ...

writes A.L. Rowse; while Jack Clemo, more austerely reflects:

Sour clay faces sunk from the dream;
Ascetic contours rasped through summer haze
Beyond the lithe corn and the poppies' blaze.
Where the unmined valley
Closed in on a nudging stream,
A few stacks loomed tall and obstinate
Beside the hidden furnace, near a field gate.

Another of these North Cornish poets, Frances Bellerby, once
summed up the Cornish situation succinctly:

The bones of this land are not speechless.
So first he should learn their language,
He whose soul, in its time-narrowed passage,
Must mirror this place.

Especially sympathetic to the Land's End region and its way
of life has been W.S. Graham, a Scottish-born poet who
settled in West Cornwall some thirty years ago, and still lives
at Madron just outside Penzance. At one time Graham was
hailed as the natural successor to Dylan Thomas, and in such
books as *The Night Fishermen* he certainly displayed the same
amazing ability at adjectival juggling. Possibly this very
romantic and lyrical poetic approach, with a vividly
unexpected juxtaposition of words achieving the same effect of
purpose as abstract painters in their field, does again help us
to see Cornwall more clearly for what it really is. These
qualities, I think, come out very clearly in a valedictory poem
which Sydney Graham wrote in memory of the famous old St
Ives fisherman painter, Alfred Wallis:

Worldhauled, he's grounded on God's great bank,
Keelheaved to Heaven, waved into boatfilled arms
Falls his homecoming leaving that old sea testament,
Watching the restless land sail rigged alongside
Townful of shallows, gulls on the sailing roofs.
And he's heaved once and for all a high dry packet
Pecked wide by curious years of a ferreting sea,
His poor house blessed by very poverty's religious
Breakwater, his past house hung in foreign galleries.
He's that stone sailor towering out of the cupboarding sea
To watch the black boats rigged by a question quietly
Ghost home and ask right out with jackets of oil
The standing white of the crew 'what hellward harbour
Bows down her seawalls to arriving home at last?'

Falls into home his prayer pray. He's there to lie
Seagreat and small, contrary and rare as sand
Sea sheller. Yes falls to me his kept beating, painted heart,
An ararat shore, loud limpet stuck to its terror,
Drags home the bible keel from a returning sea
And four black, shouting steerers stationed on movement
Call out arrival over the landgreat houseboat.
The ship of land with birds on seven trees
Calls out farewell like Melville talking down on
Nightfalls devoted barque and the parable whale.
What shipcry falls? The holy families of foam
Fall into wilderness and 'over the jasper sea.'
The gulls wade into silence. What deep seasaint
Whispered this keel out of its element?

Sometimes, of course, the visiting poet has taken a more
caustic attitude, like John Heath-Stubbs whose memorable
lines beginning 'This is a hideous and wicked country' I
quoted in Chapter I. Together with the poet David Wright,
Heath-Stubbs once lived for some years out on the cliffs at
Gurnard's Head, near Zennor, and evidently took a dim view
of local life:

Romantic Cornwall's dead and gone,
With Stephen Hawker in his tomb;
The Western Ocean breaks upon
The Land's End Point in a froth of foam –
The welter of unappeasable grief;
The artists caper in St Ives,
Where, disembarking from his leaf,
A hermit stepped from the wild waves ...

The present Poet Laureate himself, John Betjeman, has had a long-standing love affair with Cornwall, including the western end. He has in fact written many beautiful poems about the scenery and romantic nature of the county: however, he, too, has been provoked into irony:

In pools beyond the reach of tide
The Senior Service cartons glide
And on the sand the surf line lisps
With wrappings of potato crisps.
The breakers bring with merry noise
Tribute of broken plastic toys
And lichened spears of blackthorn glitter
With harvest of the August litter.
Here in the late October light
See Cornwall, a pathetic sight,
Raddled and put upon and tired
And looking somewhat over-hired,
Remembering in the autumn air
The years when she was young and fair –
Those golden and unpeopled bays,
The shadowy cliffs and sheep-worn ways,
The legions of unsurfed on surf,
The thyme and mushroom-scented turf,
The slate-hung farms, the oil-lit chapels,
Thin elms and lemon-coloured apples –
Going and gone beyond recall
Now she is free for One and All.

> One day a tidal wave will break
> Before the breakfasters awake
> And sweep the caras out to sea
> The oil the tar and you and me
> And leave in windy criss cross motion
> A waste of undulating ocean
> From which jut out, a second Scilly,
> The Isles of Roughtor and Brown Willy.

In surveying the literary connotations of Land's End, whether past or present, it increasingly becomes evident that there is a positive embarrassment of material. While there has only been space to quote a few poets it should be emphasised that many other very good poets have written about the area: Frank Ruhmrund, Richard Jenkin, Peter Redgrove, Allen Curnow, Julian Ennis and David Grubb, to mention just a few. In the same way, where I have picked upon one writer, or a small group of writers, associated with a particular part of West Cornwall, i.e. Virginia Woolf at St Ives, the Lawrences at Zennor, Laura Knight at Lamorna – it always has to be remembered that there are many other well-known writers with strong local associations. Certain places do seem to have drawn an unusual number of writers. Zennor is a good case in point, and has been dealt with – Sennen Cove, too, has been another literary centre. Even remote spots like Cape Cornwall have been vividly written about by writers of such quality as Frank Baker, Hammond Innes and Winston Graham.

Crossing to the other southern coast and passing casually through the small village of Porthcurno we pull up with a start at the realisation that here once lived Bertrand Russell – and still lives his ex-wife, Dora Russell, now in her eighties. In her autobiographical book *The Tamarisk Tree*, Dora Russell has given some memorable pictures of her early life with 'Bertie' at Porthcurno, with many literary gatherings at their house, Carn Voel. Cornwall features in some of Russell's letters but otherwise does not appear greatly in his work but Dora Russell has written quite considerably about the county she loves so much. Once in the *Cornish Review* she wrote of her delight in escaping from London to Cornwall: to a world in which the noise and fret of the city had vanished, a world of rain and shine and – timelessness.

Too easily forgotten are both the work and the wisdom of men 'That go down to the sea in ships' or live, and for all seasons, on the farms. It is of these that remote areas such as West Cornwall perpetually remind us. We need, too, the wild spaces little touched by human labour. Nowhere better than down here can one feel the mysterious link between man and the whole of his planet down to the very substance of its rocky foundations. Here I learned to respect the power of the sea, the fury of the wind, and to adore, every year afresh, fragile, young, green life springing from the brown soil. Here, though one may surmise that in aeons of time all this will come to an end, none the less, feeling myself a part of it, one with it all, I have my share in eternity. To live a life so regimented as never to know this experience is to miss something that is essential to being human.

Porthcurno, like so many other quite remote corners of West Cornwall, can boast more than a single literary association. It is the unexpected setting for one of England's most remarkable theatres – the romantically situated Minack Theatre on the cliffs at St Levan. To reach it, you walk down to Porthcurno beach through vegetation that in the summer is studded with tropical plants; over the last two hundred yards or so a cascade of white sand slopes down and disappears, like the underground transatlantic cables beneath it, into the restless waters of the Atlantic. Such a beautiful cove, an idyllic beach with great Cornish cliffs towering on either side – there is a great temptation, indeed, to stay and bask in the sunshine. However, you will notice a pathway leading from the beach up the steep side of the west cliff, joining the cliff path towards Land's End, then wandering on. Like a curious explorer you should follow this path, now sign-posted, up and up, until finally mounting some ninety granite steps you come upon an unexpected sight. Here on top of a wild and remote Cornish cliff, nearly three hundred miles from London and its theatreland, you are suddenly confronted with something bizarre and almost unbelievable – a *theatre box office*! A few steps more and your journey's end is sighted. Here on the lonely cliffs where indeed you might expect to encounter pixies and elves, even maybe a lurking giant or two, but never surely this – here, as your footsteps follow a winding pathway that zigzags down the face of the cliff with the vast canopy of the Atlantic stretching ahead – here, appearing magically and marvellously into vision is the Minack Theatre, literally hewn out of the cliffside, largely by the efforts of its owner, Miss Dorothy Cade, and her gardener, Billy Rawlings.

The Minack is a most remarkable creation, unique on the British shores, perhaps in Europe. When the well-known London producer Ernest Peirce first visited it he remarked he had never seen anything so beautiful in all his travels. 'I thought, we *cannot* let a thing like this die. Shakespeare may have known Cornwall. He must surely have written some of his plays to be played in Cornwall, for his beautiful dialogue only fits a county such as this.' True to his word Ernest Peirce moved down to Penzance and instituted a Cornish Shakespearean Festival with the Minack as headquarters. That was in 1932 – today, half a century later, not only is the Minack busy every summer season, but the remarkable Miss Cade, now in her eighties, is still around to make sure all is well.

Shakespeare, in fact, has been the favourite choice of the Minack and there have been some remarkable performances there of *The Tempest*, *Twelfth Night*, *Antony and Cleopatra*, *King Lear*, *A Midsummer Night's Dream*, *The Taming of the Shrew*, even *Othello*. Other playwrights, too, have been well represented – among them Christopher Fry, James Bridie, John Whiting, Bernard Shaw, Jean Anouilh and Norman Nicholson. Today visiting companies come from all over Britain to put on weekly performances during the summer season – among them the Cambridge University Players, the Dartington School, the

Bristol Youth Company and the Gloucestershire County Theatre Group.

Adapting plays for the Minack is one thing: writing a play specifically for that setting is something even more ambitious. This was brought off triumphantly some years ago by Bristol playwright Nora Ratcliffe, who was invited down to the Minack by Mrs Collingwood Selby, Cornwall County Drama Adviser, and drawn into a discussion of the rival merits of several versions of the Tristan legend – Hardy's *Queen of Cornwall*, John Masefield's *Tristram* and an American version.

> The theatre haunted me. Again and again we came back to a discussion of the plays and I found myself dissatisfied not with the plays themselves but with the fact they didn't fit the theatre. The Minack demanded its own play. Whatever play was put on the Atlantic would be the main actor, and none of the plays suggested gave this pride of place to the ocean ... 'Well then,' they said, 'why don't you write us one?'

The temptation proved irresistible. Mrs Ratcliffe based her version on a modern French writing of the twelfth century versions, finding in the old troubadour narratives the recurring theme of the sea. Looking back she says that everything seemed simple. She read the material with the Minack in mind; anything that didn't fit automatically dropped out of recollection. Her imagination was especially caught by the theatre of the scene where Mark hands Iseult to the Lepers. She could see Iseult moving slowly down from the top gate behind the audience. A half mad Mark stared up at her; grey lichen like shapes of lepers lay on the rocks to the audience's left. Obviously the long wall over to the right became Mark's inner castle; the entrance from the harbour had to be up the steps on the right and so on. Scene after scene unfolded itself; all that remained was to write it. Thanks to the kindness of Miss Cade, she was able to go down to the Minack and stay with her for three weeks with nothing to do but write.

Nora Ratcliffe insisted that the play couldn't have been written anywhere else but at the Minack: not only so that one could check the staging, but so that the sea, the gulls, the changing light could find their way into the imagery of the play itself – 'tilted wing of a gull, black as rock's shadow, turn through the rock teeth'.

Subsequently Mrs Ratcliffe not only produced the play but joined the chorus and shared the experience of being on the stage during a performance.

I shall never regret having done so; the joy of playing on the Minack stage; the feeling a part of the total effect, sensing the attention of the audience (even hearing the screwing back of thermos flask tops as a new scene opened) was a high reward for wearing a scratchy hessian frock and scrambling down to the dressing tent over rocky paths in the uncertain flicker of storm lanterns. At one of the early rehearsals some bright spirit suggested a midnight matinee, and the idea grew to resolution. It didn't matter if nobody came. We wanted to play the whole thing in stage lighting – perhaps that was the reason, or perhaps we knew that by the last night we should be so Minack drunk that to leave the theatre at 10.30 would be an anticlimax. So the midnight matinee was launched; to start at 11 p.m., less than an hour after the normal performance had ended. It seemed to us, as we waited for the first horn call that half Cornwall wanted to see a play at midnight; if, as someone said, we were mad, then the entire Penwith peninsula was peopled with lunatics! A black lava like stream of audience oozed down the treacherous path; pale blue programmes twinkled under pocket torches; a full moon – perhaps that explained things! – glimmered on the white head-dresses of the players; fringes of white foam sighed around the Minack Rock. The second horn-call; we each clutched our cheese, our salmon, basket of eggs, and the last performance of *Tristan of Cornwall* started. It was then I knew that for at least fifty people scattered about the shadowy rocks, the Minack Theatre, an immortal love story and the warmth of friendship engendered by mutual creation would be inextricably interwoven in a lasting memory. Thank you, Cornwall!

It would be possible to write reams more about such a unique place as the Minack – much simpler, really, for readers to go and see for themselves. Living as I do only a couple of miles away I can promise you will not be disappointed. Seldom in any other theatre can there be such pure drama about the moment when the stage lights awake and all else is shrouded in dusk and darkness. For if you are lucky it is likely that the darkness is only for a moment – that from behind a passing cloud there will come a silvery whisper of light that widens in scope until in all its glorious fullness the moonlight falls upon the wide waters of Porthcurno Bay and over the mysterious and shadowy undulations of the surrounding land.

Then indeed is your cup of wonder full, with the world of your play outlined on the spotlit green sward below, while beyond the vast backcloth of the moonlit scene stretches to the horizon, broken here and there by the flickering lights of the Newlyn fishing fleet streaming out to sea. Such moments are a pure magic, attaining a dreamlike quality: afterwards, bemused and still captivated, you will find it hard to adjust yourself back to everyday life.

It is not far from the white-washed sands of Porthcurno, past Logan Rock and the little cove of Penberth, to the wild cliffs above Lamorna Cove – and here again we are at once among literary figures. I have already referred to Ithell Colquhoun. A more famous writer who has spent the last three decades in the area is Derek Tangye, a member of an old Cornish family, one-time London journalist who some thirty years ago threw up a career in Fleet Street in order with his wife to 'get away from it all', and has lived ever since at the Minack, a beautiful daffodil farm set on the edge of the cliffs. Derek Tangye's deceptively casual tales of everyday life at his chosen rural retreat have helped to revive a tremendous interest in Lamorna, and his home appears to hold an irresistible attraction for dozens of people – readers who, captivated by his accounts, long to see the real thing. As an autobiographical writer myself I know only too well what problems such visitors can often pose, but this is undoubtedly part of the price to be paid for choosing to expose one's life in the pages of a book. Nevertheless Derek Tangye often does it with great verve: here for instance is his very first description, in *A Gull on the Roof*, of how he and his wife discovered their dream cottage:

> The path we walked along was only a shadow of a path, more like the trodden run of badgers. Here, because there was no sign of habitation, because the land and the boulders and the rocks embraced the sea without interference, we could sense we were part of the beginning of time, the centuries of unceasing waves, the unseen pattern of the wild generations of foxes and badgers, the ageless gales that had lashed the desolate land, exultant and roaring, a giant harbour of sunken ships in their wake. And we came to a point, after a steep climb, where a great Carn stood balanced on a smaller one, upright like a huge man standing on a stool, as if it were a sentinel waiting to hail the ghosts of lost sailors. The track, on the other side, had tired of the undergrowth which blocked its way along the head of the cliff, for it sheered seawards, tumbling in a zig zag course to the scarred grey rocks below. We stood on the pinnacle ... the curve of Mount's Bay leading to the Lizard Point on the left, the Wolf Rock lighthouse a speck in the distance, a French crabber a mile off shore, pale blue hull and small green sail aft, chugging through the white speckled sea towards Newlyn, and high above us a buzzard, its wings spread motionless, soaring effortlessly into the sky.
>
> Jeannie suddenly pointed inland. 'Look!' she said. 'There it is!'
>
> There was never any doubt in either of our minds. The small, grey cottage a mile away, squat on the lonely landscape, surrounded by trees and edged into the side of a hill, became as if by magic the present and the future. It

was as if a magician beside this ancient Carn had cast a spell upon us, so that we could touch the future as we could, at that moment, touch the Carn. There in the distance we could see our figures moving about our daily tasks, a thousand, thousand figures criss-crossing the untamed land, dissolving into each other, leaving a mist of excitement of our times to come.

As with most writers about West Cornwall the influence of the land's hidden and secretive powers are never far away, and in books such as *A Cat in the Window*, *A Donkey in the Meadow*, *The Way to the Minack* and *A Cottage in the Country* among the everyday chit-chat there are sensitive descriptions of the wild and lovely scenery around where he lives, an area stretching from the great strewn cove of Lamorna on the one hand, past the newly erected white lighthouse of Tater Dhu and on to Penberth Cove and the Logan Rock on the other. Tangye has a nice way, however, of always returning to base, as it were, with such an evident relief and feeling of closeness, that this in itself communicates a very deep love and understanding for the area.

> The only entrance to our cliff was through this gate to the top. It was no place for strangers. There was a deep cleft biting into the land, a sheer fall to the sea below, guarding one boundary of the meadows; and the other boundary disappeared into boulders, brambles, gorse, and in summer a forest of bracken. Below were the rocks, granite, and blue elvan pitted with fissures, huge ungainly shapes each part of the whole which sloped without plan inevitably into the sea. Here the seaweed, draped like an apron, thickened the water at low tide; the gulls, oyster catchers, and turnstones poked among it, uttering wild cries. There was the sense of loneliness and yet of greatness, this was unmanageable nature, the freedom man chooses.

In that last sentence Derek Tangye surely puts his finger on one of the clues as to why Land's End has developed into such a literary entity, almost an industry one might say. Few men, especially writers, can resist this challenge, this vision of mystery and loneliness. Sometimes, of course, the writer has come first for that alone, and not with any ideas of writing about it – the reason, one imagines, for the recent settling, also upon the Lamorna Cliffs only a mile or two from his neighbour Derek Tangye, of the famous spy writer, John le Carré. To date, so far as I know, John le Carré has not written directly about Cornwall, at least not in a novel, but not long ago he was interviewed in his Lamorna home (three old Cornish cottages converted into one imposing residence) by Melvyn Bragg for an interesting South Bank programme. I remember shots of Le Carré stalking over moors and out along the wild surf-spattered beaches which made me reflect that surely before long some of this will indeed emerge in his writings.

The Lamorna region in particular seems to have attracted an unusual number of writers in recent years. Among these are two I have already mentioned, Ithell Colquhoun, and in the past Dame Laura Knight: there have also been two other remarkable women writers, the ex-nun Monica Baldwin who for some years lived in a tiny house built into the side of the cliffs, where she wrote a minor best-seller, *I Leaped Over the Wall* – and Gwen Moffatt, a professional mountain and rock climber, who has written vividly about her years living in Cornwall in autobiographical books like *Space Below My Feet*.

Yet another woman to have written most entertainingly about Lamorna (is there something strangely feminine about the local atmosphere?) is Susan Mitchell with her *Recollections of Lamorna Cove*. This of course is essentially more of a purely local effort, but representative of a growing body of such literature epitomised by similar books put out by Muriel Sara, or Ben Batten's *History of Newlyn*, or that popular memory of life with a Mousehole fishing family, *Harbour Village* by Leo Tregenza, or Dorothy Yglesias's best selling account of running the bird hospital at Mousehole, *The Cry of a Bird*.

Perhaps it is fitting to conclude this literary survey of Land's End with a brief note on the development since the last war of an encouraging number of local publishing ventures. Just as in the mid-forties many artists and writers were glad to turn their back on the horrors and tedium of the war and flock down to Cornwall – so, inevitably, methods arose to facilitate the showing and publication of their work. More than eighty years ago 'Q', that great Cornishman and literary critic, used to edit the very erudite and entertaining *Cornish Magazine*, with an impressive list of contributors including H.D. Lowry, Charles Lee, A.K. Hamilton Jenkin, the Hocking Brothers, Stanhope Forbes, H.S. Wilmott and others.

When I myself first settled in West Cornwall, in a tiny cottage up on the side of Trencrom Hill, conveniently placed for both St Ives and Penzance as well as the whole romantic peninsula, it soon became clear to me that the time was over ripe for emulating "Q's" worthy example. In 1949, rather rashly using my own limited funds, I launched the first *Cornish Review* whose declared aim was 'to fulfil an obvious need – to provide a platform for discussing and analysing cultural activities in Cornwall, along with an outlet for new poetry and fiction by writers of Cornish descent or living in Cornwall'.

I can remember how we drew up a prospectus and for night after night my wife and I sat by the oil lamp in our cottage folding up the leaflets, inserting them in envelopes and sending them off to a whole variety of Cornwall-lovers both at home and abroad. The magazine was to be published quarterly and the contents would total 96 pages including 12 pages of photographs. We mailed some 500 prospectuses and within a week or two accumulated 200 annual subscriptions. We felt proudly we were on our way ... And indeed in due course the magazine appeared and was warmly welcomed, especially by Howard Spring who, declaring it to be the duty of Cornish men and women to support this new venture, said it was only fitting that the region should have a place for uttering its own voice, 'for it is a region of character and idiosyncrasy. Its people and climate and their interaction have produced something easily distinguished from anything that will be found elsewhere; and this is true despite the levelling consequences of our day. So long as that remains true there will be a reason for a magazine like this.'

Looking back now, Howard Spring's praise seems not unreasonable, for among our early contributions were such items as: 'My World as a Potter' by Bernard Leach, 'Ben Nicholson' by J.P. Hodin, 'The Hocking Brothers' by Jack Clemo, 'The Cornish Gorsedd' by R. Morton Nance, 'Serenade to a Cornish Fox' by Charles Causley, 'Memories of Cornwall's Art Colonies' by Charles Marriott, and 'Early Cornish Railways' by David St John Thomas. Not a bad batch for a remote little regional magazine!

After four years, alas, the first *Cornish Review* came to an untimely end but this was purely through lack of financial support and I always felt sure in my heart that the phoenix would rise again – and so it did in 1966, supported now by a small but vital grant from the South West Arts Council. This time we were able to produce 27 consecutive issues over eight productive years and I think it would be fair to say that in this 'second life', the *Cornish Review* helped quite considerably in encouraging many of the writers with whom this book has been concerned. Once again I think we were fortunate in being able to boast a contents list of a level of which many a national literary magazine might have been proud – for instance, 'The Loneliness of Jack Clemo' by Ernest Martin, 'Howard Spring and Cornwall' by his widow, Marion Howard Spring, 'The Work of Peter Lanyon' by Michael Canney, 'Sir Richard Carew' by F.E. Halliday, 'The Minack Theatre' by Frank Ruhrmund, 'The Brontes: Grand-Daughters of Cornwall' by Ida Proctor, 'A Note on Mary Butts' by Frank Baker, 'The du Mauriers' by Noel Welch, 'The Plays of Donald Rowe' by Paul Newman, stories by Ronald Duncan, C.C. Vyvyan, Mary Williams, James Turner and Rosalind Wade, and poems by Jack Clemo, Charles Causley, D.M. Thomas, John Betjeman, W.S. Graham and Arthur Caddick (plus reproductions of paintings by Patrick Heron, Bryan Wynter, Bryan Pearce, Mary Jewells, John Miller, Barbara Hepworth, Terry Frost, John Wells and John Milne).

Unfortunately, as with the first series, the second *Cornish*

Review was forced to cease publication early in the 1970's. By then I like to think it had helped to create a favourable literary climate in the county for although no other Cornish literary magazine has as yet made an appearance, during the past decade there have developed an impressive number of local publishing houses devoted largely to books about the Land's End area. The largest among these is the most romantically placed – Sydney Sheppard's United Writers' Publishing Company which not only publishes but actually prints a wide list of books from its headquarters at lovely Trevail Mill, down a wandering farm track off the moorland road from St Ives to Zennor, within sight and sound of the gulls that hover around Seal Island. Then there is Bossinney Books, another local publishing venture which has expanded impressively since its founder Michael Williams, first hit on the idea while living at Lamorna Cove – among its local titles the *Ross Poldark Story* by David Clarke, *St Just-in-Penwith* by Frank Ruhrmund, *Penzance to Land's End* by Michael Williams, and *My Cornwall*, with Penwith contributions from Derek Tangye, Arthur Caddick, Denys Val Baker, C.C. Vyvyan and Margo Maeckleberghe. Three individual Penzance ventures into publishing have been made by Peter Dalwood, a local bookseller who brought out a reprint of *A Week in the Land's End*, by Reg Watkiss, a local photographer who published a unique collection of photographs of *Old Newlyn*, and by Peter Pool, author of the official *History of Penzance* who was published a number of important booklets, like one about the Cornish language, *The Death of Cornish*.

From further afield Donald Rawe's Lodenek Press at Padstow has published several books about the Land's End area (they also issue the official Mebyon Kernow literature) while D.M. Bradford Barton's of Truro, through their Tor Mark Press, have been responsible for *Cornwall's Atlantic Coast*, *Tales of the Cornish Smugglers*, *The Story of St Ives* and other local volumes. Although not operating inside Cornwall the Barracuda Press have produced an ambitious series of historical portraits of Cornish towns, including *The Book of St Ives* by Cyril Noall: and one or two national publishers with a

special interest in the West Country – notably William
Kimber Ltd., and David and Charles Ltd., – have published a
wide range of books that include coverage of Land's End.

A Literary Gazetteer

To Land's End

Hayle

Set on the edge of the wide estuary which leads to the
mysterious rolling hills of Penwith, Hayle has always been
regarded as the main entry point to the magic kingdom. At
first sight the town may not seem exciting but in fact it has
intriguing back streets down which stand many lovely old
Georgian-style houses that were once the homes of the 'copper
barons', men who made their fortunes from local mining. In
one of these houses for some years lived Compton Mackenzie,
probably the best-known author to be associated with the
district.

There have been local writers, too – and some years ago
Edmund Vale produced a well documented official history of
Harvey and Co., the large firm who until recently seemed to
own not merely the entire harbour but also other parts of the
town. From Hayle you can walk out along those famous 'three
miles of golden sands' that lead to such beauty spots as Nell's
Mouth and Gwithian, with the whiteness of the Godrevy
Lighthouse nearby, an area written about by Francis Kilvert
and Virginia Woolf and, more recently, by local authoress
Erma Harvey James.

When they lived on the other side of the estuary at Carbis
Bay Havelock Ellis and his wife often caught the little rowing
boat ferry to Hayle on walking expeditions along the coast. It
is the estuary, now preserved for all time, it is hoped, as a bird
sanctuary, that gives Hayle its rather unusual character.
Standing there, looking over the vast mud flats to the full glory

of the peninsula beyond, makes a good beginning to exploring
Land's End.

Lamorna Cove

Perhaps the best known of several beautiful coves indenting
the coast from Penzance round to Land's End this small
village is renowned both for its artistic and literary
connections. When the Newlyn School painters settled in the
area at the turn of the century many of them rented or bought
houses along the straggling valley leading to the cove – among
them Ernest and Dod Procter, Harold and Laura Knight,
Lamorna Birch, T.C. Gotch, Alfred Munnings, etc. Both
Laura Knight and Sir Alfred Munnings produced books, as
did some of the visitors to the cove – among them W.M.
Davies, author of *The Autobiography of a Super Tramp*. Crosbie
Garstin, son of the painter, Normal Garstin, and himself
author of the best-selling trilogy, *The Owl's House*, lived there;
so at various times did Monica Baldwin, the ex-nun who
wrote *I Leaped Over the Wall*, Gwen Moffatt, climber and
mountaineer and author of *Space Beneath My Feet*, and Ithell
Colquhoun, author of *The Living Stones*. Today the two authors
most closely associated with Lamorna Cove (by a strange
chance they are near neighbours out along the lovely cliffs) are
Derek Tangye, author of *A Gull on the Roof*, *A Donkey in the
Meadow*, *The Way to the Minack* and other best selling
autobiographical books, and John Le Carré, world famous for
The Spy Who Came In From The Cold, *Tinker Tailor Soldier Spy*,
and other tales of espionage.

Land's End

So many writers have visited this landmark that to list them
all would be impossible. Quite a substantial minority came

back to settle in the area, usually at nearby Sennen Cove which has been the home of Mary Butts, Arthur Symons, Ruth and George Manning Sanders, among others. At first sight on a busy day the visitor to Land's End may be put off by the sight of rows of motor coaches, car parks thronged with motors and what may look like a sea of milling tourists. However it is worth persevering and wandering out along the cliffs in search of both solitude and beauty. Despite all the commercial blemishes few people have ever regretted visiting this unique place. If you haven't been able to make such a visit then read the poems of Tennyson and Swinburne or the memories of Charles Dickens and Wilkie Collins, or of naturalists such as W.H. Hudson and J.F. Blight. There seems no end to the literature about Land's End – just as there is no real end to the place itself. A large hotel stands on the point at Land's End but more cosy is the local pub, the First and Last at Sennen, or the Old Success Inn down in Sennen Cove – while, of course, the Cove is on the edge of one of Cornwall's most famous surfing bays, Whitesands. At Land's End and Sennen alike the visitor can stare out dreamily across the Atlantic swell towards the distant Scilly Isles, well able to believe in the famous legend of the lost land of Lyonesse.

Mousehole

A small and picturesque fishing village set on the edge of Mount's Bay Mousehole has inspired many painters, including in recent times Adrian Ryan, Jack Pender, Jean Gilchrist, Biddy Picard, George Lambourne. Writers have often stayed in the village, Dylan Thomas, for instance. It is not generally known, but near the end of his life the American novelist, John Steinbeck, spent a winter there while working on a planned book on King Arthur. On a less happy note John Davidson, the nineteenth century poet, was found drowned off the little port after taking his own life. Small though it is (snug is the better word) Mousehole is well-equipped with two good pubs, The Ship and The Coastguards, and a restaurant at the water's edge, the Lobster Pot. Many interesting old buildings are to be found among the many winding cobbled streets – one of which leads up to the famous Mousehole Bird Hospital, whose founder, Dorothy Yglesias, wrote a best-seller, *The Cry of a Bird*. Leo Tregenza is another local author – his *Harbour Village* is a fascinating introduction to the life of a small fishing village.

Nancledra

Set almost exactly half way between St Ives and Penzance and with views of both coasts, Nancledra is a village more important than its straggling outline might suggest. It is in fact quite large, taking in numerous diversionary side lanes which lead to remote areas with such romantic names as Georgia. Perhaps because of its convenient access to both sides of the peninsula the village has always been a favourite spot for writers who prefer living tucked away from the towns. Best known of the literary figures associated with Nancledra has been West Cornwall's Poet Laureate, Arthur Caddick, now in his seventies but still writing weekly poems for the local newspaper, the *Cornishman*. It was he who once pointed out that the village is part of 'a majestic barricade which seals off the prehistoric interior of Land's End'. Nancledra's single pub, the Engine Inn, has been the scene of many convivial gatherings of painters and poets. Sven Berlin, the sculptor turned author, once lived opposite the Engine Inn. During another period John Antrobus, author of *The Bed Sitting Room*, had a cottage nearby.

Newlyn

Now the second largest fishing port in the West Country Newlyn is very much a working town, and every day the long fish quays are thronged with fishing boats, sometimes as many as two hundred. It is a port full of atmosphere and the smell of tar and fish and has made a favourite setting for many well-known paintings, especially those done by the large group of the Newlyn School who set up there at the turn of the century (among them Stanhope Forbes, T.C. Gotch, Frank Bramley, Norman Garstin, Walter Langley). At the centre of the art colony stands the Passmore Edwards Gallery which receives a large subsidy from the Arts Council of Great Britain. Here in addition to exhibitions there are literary debates and poetry readings (Charles Causley, Jack Clemo and Peter Redgrove among recent appearances).

Life at Newlyn has featured in *The Magic of a Line* by Laura Knight, in *Twenty Years at St Hilary* by Bernard Walke, and in the novels of Charles Lee such as *The Widow Woman*. Potters and painters, poets and novelists all mingle happily in the town's colourful pubs, the Tolcarne, the Swordfish, the Star, the Red Lion and the Fisherman's Arms, and there are several good restaurants such as the Smugglers and the Tolcarne. In this day of modernisation and tourism gone mad Newlyn has somehow managed to remain refreshingly unspoiled – the sort of place St Ives was before commercialism took over.

Penzance

As befits the 'capital' of West Cornwall Penzance is a large and gracious town set rather beautifully along the edge of Mount's Bay and boasting many areas – Chapel Street, Morrab Road, Morrab Place – of character. It has the semi-tropical Morrab Gardens in which is set the unique private Morrab library, as well as Penlee Park where art exhibitions are held, and there is an art school and a large public library. The town abounds with antique shops and pubs – there are reputed to be 39 of each! – and with its large number of hotels and guesthouses makes an ideal centre for touring West

Cornwall. If you come down by train anyway you can't go further, as the rail track ends at Penzance! – though if you wish you can take the Scillonian steamer (or helicopter) to the Scilly Isles.

Among authors associated with Penzance over the years have been Dr William Borlase, Davies Gilbert, Humphry Davy, J.F. Blight, J.C. Tregarthern, John Davidson, W.H. Hudson, Wallace Nichols. Today a town of contrasts – big supermarkets vying with health food shops and craft markets – Penzance retains a strong identity of its own, 'the town on a hill' (basically it is set round Market Jew Street which climbs up to where the statue of the town's favourite son, Humphry Davy, looks out over Mount's Bay). Well known writers and artists lecture at the thriving West Cornwall Arts Centre and there are frequent performances of plays and opera at the St John's Hall. A good town for retiring to!

Porthcurno

Set in the lovely bay bordered by the Logan Rock in the east and St Levan in the west, this village is notable for three features: its beautiful white sandy beach, its unique Minack Theatre hewn into the side of the cliffs, and being the headquarters of the Cable and Wireless Company, from where cables stretch out under the sea to the Continent. There are lovely cliff walks including one that ends up at the ancient church of St Levan (intrepid climbers can carry on via Porthgwarra and Nanjizel to Land's End). Literary-wise most of Porthcurno's associations have been through the Minack Theatre, to which have come many well known actors and actresses (during the war Margaret Lockwood, Patricia Roc and Stewart Granger filmed there for *Love Story*). However one house at Porthcurno has special literary associations and that is Carn Voel, home for half a century of Dora Russell, now in her eighties and author of several books including her recent autobiographical *The Tamarisk Tree* – and of course earlier this century, when they were still married, her husband, the philosopher Bertrand Russell, also lived and did some of his writing there.

Sancreed

J.C. Tregarthen, who wrote many marvellous nature books about animal life out at Land's End, once stayed at Sancreed which, although a tiny hamlet, has a long history. It lies just off the main road from Penzance to Land's End and makes a convenient stopping off point for the walker. Today there remains the historic old church and just a few cottages and farms, but somehow the village retains a strong social life. Painter John Miller and the potter Michael Truscott live at the Old Vicarage, where there is much literary and artistic activity. In many ways Sancreed is representative of several such remote villages in West Cornwall – New Mill being another. It is the sort of place in which one is quite likely, down some remote land, to find a poet working away diligently in an old converted cottage. T. Craske Rising, once famous as headmaster of the Humphry Davy Grammar School, Penzance, in the days when it was rated about fourth best in the country, lives on the outskirts, and writes and lectures. If you set out to find Sancreed do not be surprised if you get lost and end up at a tiny hamlet called Grumbla ... That's all part of the fun of exploring the Land's End peninsula (which by the way at Sancreed takes in Carn Euny, a prehistoric site with several *fougous*.)

St Buryan

One of the oldest villages in Cornwall, with a church going back to before King Athelstan, St Buryan acts as the focus point for the south west tip of the Land's End peninsula. Its church has quite a famous history written about in great detail by the Reverend Croft Hooper, a previous incumbent, and published as a local booklet – not always to everyone's liking as there have been rumours of hauntings and evil spirits. (Aleister Crowley is supposed to have conducted a black mass there once). Only recently a granddaughter of Dora Russell tragically set fire to herself and burned to death in the churchyard – St Buryan was also the locality chosen for the controversial sadistic film, *Straw Dogs*. While no authors of note appear to have lived in the centre of the village, technically its area of influence extends to Derek Tangye and John Le Carré over at Lamorna and includes Sir Darrell Bates, a retired diplomatist author of several novels, at Crean, and Dora Russell at Porthcurno. It is also my own home area and at our old mill at Tresidder I have written numerous Cornish autobiographical books and novels.

St Ives

Best known as Britain's art colony by the sea St Ives was originally very much a working fishing port with more than 100 boats. Today the fishing is almost gone, superseded by 'trips round the bay', and much of the town's atmosphere blemished by trappings of tourism (including car parks everywhere). Fortunately not even these ravages can spoil the sheer beauty of the town's situation and it is this which has drawn, and will continue to draw both artists and writers. Painters have been more to the fore – Ben Nicholson, Peter Lanyon, Barbara Hepworth, Patrick Heron, Bryan Wynter, Bryan Pearce. Writers connected with the town have in fact often been painters with an extra gift for words, such as Sven Berlin, the sculptor. Virginia Woolf, Guy Thorne, F.E. Halliday, Mary Williams, Cyril Noall, Norman Levine, W.S. Graham, Bernard Leach, have all featured St Ives in their books. As a place to stay in, the town is well-equipped with

hotels and guest houses as well as hundreds of Bed and
Breakfast cottages – The Sloop, a pub on the wharf's edge, is
world famous, its walls heavily hung with drawings and
paintings by artists of the town, and there are other cosy pubs
and half a dozen good restaurants. Best trips across the bay,
walks along Clodgy cliffs, surfing on Porthmeor Beach – these
are many reasons apart from literary ones to justify a visit to
St Ives.

St Just

Often called St Just-in-Penwith to distinguish it from St Just-
in-Roseland, near Falmouth, this town also takes in England's
only cape, Cape Cornwall. Essentially a mining town and
close by Cornwall's oldest working mine at Geevor, St Just is
grey and dark and very Cornish in atmosphere. It is a place
where old customs have been preserved – notably the annual
St Just Feast Day, a great occasion for local celebrations. In
recent years owing to steep rises in house prices elsewhere
there has been quite a movement of people out to St Just,
including artists and writers who snapped up some of the
many empty cottages that used to lie around. Painters as well
as potters and weavers are to be found working in St Just.
Writers associated with the town seem to come and go – in the
past it has been used as a setting by R.M. Ballantyne, author
of *Coral Island* and other boys' tales, and more recently by
Hammond Innes. Frank Baker, author of several novels about
Cornwall as well as a delightful personal guidebook, *The Call
of Cornwall*, spent some years at Kenidzhak Valley, near Cape
Cornwall. Poets have been drawn continually to the dramatic
cliff scenery, especially where it combines with ruined mines,
as at Botallack (D.M. Thomas, the Cornish poet, has written
beautifully of this spot). With five pubs within a few yards of
each other around the town square, as well as snug pubs and
restaurants out at nearby Pendeen and Trewellard and
Botallack, St Just remains very much a community of its own.

Zennor

Few villages in Cornwall can boast so many literary connections and the stories are told in this book of how D.H. Lawrence and his wife, Middleton Murry and Katherine Mansfield, Virginia Woolf and others were drawn to the unforgettable, lonely moorland scenery in which the village is set. With its Norman church and pub, Tinner's Arms, almost side by side in the little central hollow Zennor can be seen as the archetypical Cornish village. Apart from the interesting folk museum just past the pub the village's main attractions are the surrounding scenery, and there are magnificent walks both up to the moors and down to the sea (then taking the National Trust path along to Gurnard's Head, the next hamlet, where the local pub of that name was a famous literary centre during the 60's and 70's).

To this day Zennor's literary flavour remains strong: at Eagle's Nest, a remarkable house rearing up to one side of the approach road from St Ives, painter and art critic Patrick Heron lives. Down through the village a small lane leads out to Carn Cobbla, cliffside home of author Eric Quayle who is also a book collector with a library of some 10,000 books, including many first editions. In another direction, at Trevail Mill, editor Sydney Sheppard runs his own publishing company, United Writers. Poets of the stature of John Heath-Stubbs, George Barker, David Wright and Sydney Graham have all lived and worked at Zennor, and it appears likely to remain the sort of romantic spot from which, periodically, new literary work will emerge.

Index